The Quantum Dating Club Presents

# Why Real Women Drink Straight Tequila

## The Tao of Intimacy

Sarina Stone & R. Mordant Mahon
Certified Universal Healing Tao
Instructors

drink 🙂 smart

Logo illustration by Rachel Tribble ©Rachel Tribble 2004
Cover Art by James Kilgore
Layout and Design by James Kilgore.
Second Printing: August 2010
Library of Congress Catalog Card: Pending

US ISBN (13): 978-0-9826384-2-2

Please contact The Quantum Dating Club at www.QuantumDatingClub.com
to purchase autographed copies and merchandise.
Do not participate in or encourage piracy of copyrighted materials.
Your support of the author's rights is appreciated

Hornitos™ Resposado Tequila property of:
SAUZA TEQUILA IMPORT COMPANY
TEQUILA SAUZA S.A. DE C.V.
FRANCISCO JAVIER DAUZA MORE #80
COL. CENTRO TEQUILA, JALISCO, MEXICO

# Why Real Women Drink Straight Tequila

## The Tao of Intimacy
### A Handbook For Dating In The New Millennium

## Sarina Stone & R. Mordant Mahon
### Certified Universal Healing Tao Instructors

drink smart

This writing is dedicated
to the Tao and our teacher
Master Mantak Chia

# Acknowledgements

The authors wish to thank the following for their kind contributions:

Rachel Tribble, for her generous heart and artistic talent. We love our logo!

Sauza Hornitos™ Tequila and Aimee S., for the wonderful recipes, faith and support.

Eric Thurnbeck, Steven D., Rosie H., Madam Rujah, Dorothy Gayle, Gidget H., Damon Barr, Dana McCain, Katie W. and Tony T. for donating wonderful material.

Melissa Fenech for editorial assistance.

Kay Kinsey for a fabulous MySpace page. Sherri Brault at www.SherriDesign.com for fantastic web design on TaoLady.com and QuantumDatingClub.com.

Doug Kondziolka, Alex B., Steve Morrow and Daniel A. for their contributions to the accompanying screen play.

H. Christine Lindblom, Jeanne, John, and everyone at The Authors' Press for their hard work.

**A very special thank you to
Master Mantak Chia and Universal Healing Tao,
for showing us**

# The Way.

# Contents

drink smart

# Letter from a Friend

Let me just say I am excited, I am elated, I am filled to the rim with high-octane joy. I am absolutely on fire, at the peak, at the pinnacle, at the point of no return. I have put to rest the corpse, the shell, the shadow of a man I used to be, and I am finally – after 30 years of fumbling my way through this incredible gift from God – awakened. And yes, my friend, what has been unleashed is nothing less than one of the most incredible, artistic, creative entities this planet has ever seen. My name will be encapsulated in the annals of history as one of the greatest artisan luthiers to ever ply the trade. But the story doesn't end there – it's just the beginning.

I suppose I should introduce myself since we have never actually met. I was born with the name Damon Alan Barr, and I extend to you the opportunity of making sure that you are firmly strapped into your seat and the tray is in the upright position. For you are taxiing down the runway of my cerebral cortex and about to penetrate the conventional barrier. You may feel a slight sting at the base of your spine as your essential energies enter your sacral hiatus on their journey to the mouth of God, where we will have a short layover before returning to our final destination.

We hope you are prepared to ingest solid food because there is no milk in our hold, and we strongly suggest that all weapons, apprehensions, and inhibitions be disposed of prior to your journey as you will need them not. For, inside you will find only what you take with you.

Breathe deeply three times.

Imagine yourself in a perfect place where harmony and bliss reside hand-in-hand in a single, glorious union fused together for all eternity. Words like famine, war, disease, and greed are nothing more than unfamiliar mumblings. The roses are  always in bloom; their sweet perfume hangs in the air as the virtuoso of the concert that plays continually upon all of your senses. There is only spring, and the warm rain you summon serves only to soothe you even more deeply than you could comprehend before

i

its arrival. You tread effortlessly across the lipid pools, which have formed beneath your feet. As you gaze down into them, they reflect an opulent, blue sky and you – the perfect being that stands between them.

Slowly, you extend your arms above your head and touch the tips of your fingers together as you plunge yourself into the fluid mirror. You propel effortlessly through the crystalline liquid, which you draw into your lungs, allowing it to fill your whole entity with the eternal *now* engulfing you. As you twist, turn, roll, and glide in your aquatic paradise, the sound of a single drum beats its way through the din. And then, in a single moment, the dam bursts and your paradise drains away. An unseen force pushes you to leave the glorious place you call home.

Suddenly, a blinding red light fills your eyes, and your ears overflow with the sounds of painful screams. You can't breathe. You can't see. You can't speak. You are powerless against the gigantic hands now firmly grasping your head and pulling you from your perfect place of peace. You are in trouble. You are in pain. You are afraid.

The screaming only grows louder and more frantic, and you wish it would all just stop. Just as you're free of the initial pain, hands reach out to grab you by your feet, and you are assaulted by a massive, unseen creature. Cold air rushes into your lungs as you scream out your discontented frustration at whoever is responsible for this cruel and merciless treatment. Tubes shoved into your nose violently extract the fluid that had given you life only moments before.

Finally, in a state of utter exhaustion you are laid down. And, once again, your ears fill with the beautiful din of the drum – your only friend.

Congratulations. You have just been born.

With loving gratitude,
Damon VanderBarr
www.VanderbarrViolins.com

# Sarina's Introduction

Greetings fellow sojourners on the dating path. Nice to meet you. My name is Sarina Stone, and I am a certified Universal Healing Tao Instructor – a title I am proud to hold. I received my Taoist training under the direct supervision of a Taoist Master named Mantak Chia. I have never been married, but I have been in love . . . a few times.

I began writing this book a lifetime ago as a vent for frustrations and an opportunity to humiliate those who had hurt my feelings. Today, as I read the material from my past, I see that the choices I made as a young lady – and I use the term loosely – were self-destructive, fear-based, and ignorant. I see that, at the core, I was an intelligent young girl who simply did not understand the principles of manifestation and co-creation with the Universe. I see that I was living into a negative belief system. I see that *no one did it to me* – I did it to myself.

I have no remorse for my past. Rather, I dance joyfully in the rain of my experience and carry no ill will toward those who crossed my bitter path in those days of painful passion, and hope they feel the same. I thank them for being signposts to the road I'm on now.

These pages are filled with stories and insights that have brought me to the simple reality I choose to live in today; it's nothing serious, it's just my life.

A long time ago, in a land far, far away, there was a beautiful Jewish American Princess. She had long, flowing dark hair, big brown eyes, and a voluptuous figure. She was raised in a clean, controlled, suburban ivory tower. She rode her horses across flowing fields (English saddle, of course) and was well versed in the classics and theater.

Until the 80's.

Then the shit hit the fan. She moved to Los Angeles, bought a leather mini skirt, and cropped the top of her now yellow hair. She wore ankle socks with her very high heels and a spiked dog collar.

Princess began dating. And dating. And dating. And dating. Boy, did she date.

By the time she was 22, she was haggard, bitter, and a convicted felon. She had no real connection to anyone, male or female. Even those who loved her could not get close to her.

How did our Princess go from fabulous to infamous? I can tell you. She was a train wreck just waiting to happen. She never saw herself as the glorious creature others perceived her to be. She was secretly terrified, out of control, out of touch, and really pissed off. She saw herself as the little girl whose daddy left when she was a babe, and as the inconvenience her bitter, unstable mother could not identify with. As a child she saw that women are mean, manipulative, and dishonest. And men are scoundrels who ultimately leave.

Her young mind translated the ill behaviors of those around her. She learned that bad things happen to good people and no one cares. In this world, it's kill or be killed. So she became a predator. She hunted the streets of LA looking for prey, just like the guys. She loved 'em and left 'em, just like the guys. She was the first one out the door after sex and the last one to call the next day. She became the very thing she loathed – one of *THEM.*

As luck would have it, she got arrested for selling psychedelics and marijuana. It was the best thing that ever happened to her. On her way to the "big house," an officer said, "Did it ever cross your mind that you could sell some of that stuff to someone who believes they could fly, and then jumps off a roof?" You could have knocked Princess over with a feather. No. She never actually thought about it that way. This was the first day of the rest of her life. Now, if she could just get through this imprisonment ordeal, she would make a change and redeem herself. And she did.

Fast-forward two years. A move to a cleaner town and a very humbling day job later, our Princess was making her comeback. Relocated to the American Midwest, she had become the Fairy God Manager for a small musical theater company. She was on a new path.

The artistic director for the company appeared one day with a cassette and corresponding book (on Taoist Methods of Transforming Stress into Vitality) written by Taoist Master Mantak Chia. He had paid fifty cents for the lot. Little did she know, six years later she would become one of Master Chia's favorite instructors, the President of Chi Kids Incorporated (a non-profit that serves families and children by teaching natural health), a loving family member and friend, a world traveler, an avid lover of the Tao, and the author of this text.

I hope you enjoy reading this book as much as Mordant and I enjoyed writing it.

Sarina Stone, Certified Universal Healing Tao Instructor
Director, www.ChiFamily.com, President, Chi Kids Incorporated

# Mordant's Introduction

When Sarina first started writing this book oh so many years ago, it began as a forum in which she could safely vent her frustrations at dating, at the men in her life, and at her own lack of intimacy. She had the quips, quick-witted responses, and the latest psychobabble hypothesis to back up whichever point she was making at the time.

Now, many years later, she returns to finish her dissertation only to find herself a different woman. The ignorant, pissed-off girl from the last millennium has become a grounded compassionate woman through experience and through the Tao. She has transformed herself and now brings a refreshing point of view to the table. It is this woman that became my first Taoist instructor.

And so, this is not to be a book on how men suck. Not entirely. And that's where I come in. Like Sarina, I am an instructor with Universal Healing Tao and a writer. I don't have a doctorate in psychology, but I do have one very important qualification that allows me to comment on the forthcoming material: I'm a guy. And with that "guydom" comes a guy's perspective.

Let's just launch right into the truth. I have been single all my life. I've dated. I have been the romantic and I have been the scoundrel. I've had one-night stands - many of them. As a child, I was sexually abused (not by my parents). Are these truths related? Yes, but not entirely. I know now that I am ultimately responsible for the depth of intimacy in my relationships . . . or lack thereof.

How can a man who's never been in a long-term relationship speak about intimacy? Read on and I'll tell you.

When I discovered the Tao, I saw a lack of intimacy with myself. Since then, I've spent years cleaning up my act physically, emotionally, and energetically. I have put Taoist philosophy into practice, and it has changed my day-to-day life and my interpersonal relationships.

Today, I am more intimate with myself, and this allows deeper intimacy with others.

In keeping with my proactive lifestyle, I have sought therapy to come to terms with my childhood abuse. I traveled to Tao Garden, in Thailand, and studied the art of self-transformation with Master Mantak Chia. Like a recovering drug addict shares his healing experience with fellow users, I am offering my humanity to this book. I'm not perfect, but I am conscious.

Today, I consciously create my reality - I choose to follow my dreams.

Too many of us opt for a life of mediocrity. Some even sink so low as to accept pain as the norm. In reality, there are no victims here. It is up to us to claim responsibility for our own heaven and hell. Let's face it, wallowing in a pigsty can be relaxing from time to time. (Mud bath, anyone?) But, eventually, we have to hose off and get back to work if we want to have a great life.

I believe that people can take a stand and make a difference in their own lives. This is why I am on board for this project.


R. Mordant Mahon
Certified Universal Healing Tao Instructor
Co-Founder of the Quantum Dating Club

# Hornitos™ Paloma

## OR

## Sarina's Favorite New Paradigm in Drinking

A refreshing, thirst quenching cocktail, the Paloma is the signature drink of Hornitos™, especially in Mexico. It's smooth and lively with just a splash of fizz, and one of the most pleasurable tequila drinks when made with Hornitos™.

1 part Hornitos™ Reposado Tequila
1 1⁄2 parts grapefruit soda or 1⁄2 part grapefruit juice
3⁄4 part tonic
Squeeze of lime wedge

Fill glass with ice. Pour in ingredients and stir. Garnish with lime wedge or twist, add the company of a good friend for the perfect finishing touch.

# Chapter 1

## THE QUANTUM PHYSICS
## OF DATING

### You Are What You Believe To Be True
### —or—
### Taking Responsibility For
### Your Own Shit

The new paradigm in thinking for the independent person of the millennium is that we ultimately manifest, on the physical plane, what we believe to be true. William James (1842-1910) - psychologist, philosopher, and founder of the movement of thought called Pragmatism - said, "We become what we think about most of the time. The greatest revolution in our generation is the discovery that human beings, by changing the inner attitudes of their minds, can change the outer aspects of their lives."

What we focus on matters. We affect what we concentrate on, even if only on a subatomic level. In scientific experiments, we find that light moves in waves . . . until the point where scientists choose to observe it. Then it becomes particles. So, is light a wave . . . or particles? It is both. Welcome to one of the paradoxes of Quantum Physics. As waves, electrons or photons (particles of light) have no precise location, but exist as "probability fields." As particles, the probability field "collapses" into a particle and can be located.

**Amazingly, what seems to make the difference is observation or measurement. Unmeasured, unobserved electrons behave as waves. As soon as we subject them to observation in an experiment, they "collapse" into a particle and can be located.** [1]

Strangely enough, what we observe we affect, just in the simple act of paying attention. How much more will we influence our reality when we focus all our attention, all our energies on any matter we choose?

**We are not simply bystanders on a cosmic stage; we are shapers and creators living in a participatory universe.**

John Wheeler[2]

Quantum Manifestation tells us that the quality and intention behind the thoughts inside each of us guides the outcome of our efforts out here. Documentaries like, *What The Bleep Do We Know?* and *The Secret* ask us to consider what thoughts are made of. Complex medical equipment such as an electroencephalograph (EEG) show us that when we have a thought, the brain emits a wave. We can see that when this wave hits an object, there are changes on an atomic and subatomic level in and around the object we focus on. So, what are thoughts made of that allows them to facilitate change on a molecular level?

Early Taoists were aware that thoughts are energy and used the word "Chi" to describe that energy.

**The Chi is the primordial life force itself. It begins in human life with the piercing of an egg by a sperm cell. From this original fusion, an enormously complex new human being develops. "Chi" is the continuous flow of energy linking the various tissues, organs and brain functions into a unified whole – a person.**[3]

---

1    *What the Bleep Do We Know!?*, page 57 (William Arntz, Betsy Chasse and Mark Vicente, Health Communications, Inc., 2005)

2    John Wheeler was a colleague of Albert Einstein and Niels Bohr. He also coined the term 'black hole.'

3    *Awaken Healing Energy Through The Tao*, pages 1-2 (Mantak Chia & Maneewan Chia, Aurora Press, 1983)

*Chi Kung* literally means energy work. From this point forward, we will follow the Chinese tradition, and use Chi as energy. Very chic. Very PC. But, let's not stop with philosophy. Let us explore religion as well . . .

**All that we are is the result of what we have thought. The mind is everything. What we think, we become.**

Buddha

**". . . I tell you the truth, if you have faith as small as a mustard seed, you can say to this mountain, 'Move from here to there' and it will move. Nothing will be impossible for you."**

Matthew 17:20

**Mind (as well as metals and elements) may be transmuted, from state to state; degree to degree; condition to condition; pole to pole; vibration to vibration. True Hermetic Transmutation is a Mental Art.**

The Kybalion

What this means for you and your romantic situation is that when we believe in something, it's real. Let me repeat. When we believe in something, it is real. But, how is this so? How can we change our reality? How can we "reach out and touch" something not a part of us with our mind?

Everything is interconnected on a molecular level. As previously stated, consciousness affects reality simply by becoming attentive. What happens on the inside affects your outer world. Thought becomes reality. Chi is real. Imagination and creativity are the building blocks of tomorrow. You can't see a radio wave, but you accept that it is real.

Have you ever thought about an old friend for a day or two and then picked up the phone to hear them on the other end? Did distance have anything to do with the ability to manifest or contact your friend? The invisible truth is that we are all energetically interconnected and distance, however great, does not matter.

Quantum nonlocality proves that "particles that were once together in an interaction remain, in some sense, parts of a single system which responds together to further interactions" (Gribbin, 1984). Since the entire universe originated in a flash of light known as the Big Bang, the existence of quantum nonlocality points toward a profound cosmological holism and suggests that if everything that ever interacted in the Big Bang maintains its connection with everything it interacted with, then every particle in every star and galaxy that we can see "knows" about the existence of every other particle.

–Jurgen[4]

It is important to know that the stronger the thought, the stronger the manifestation.

**Q.** What makes a thought strong?

**A.** The intention behind the thought. The mental energy, or Chi, is an important determining factor in the speed and strength of a manifestation from thought to matter.

That's why millions of people around the world practice Chi Kung. Clean up, cultivate, refine, and grow your Chi, and the world is a far more malleable place. Learn to transform your negative Chi into positive vitality and the world is your playground. Project hate and other negative thoughts onto others and hell manifests on earth – just for you.

If you want to know what you believe to be true about intimacy and dating, just look at your current romantic situation. This is your reality manifested.

For those who like to argue, I ask why? Why would you want it to be any other way? Is it less agreeable to have the option of keeping or improving your situation? Do you want to be a victim, surfing the uncertain waves of creation or would you rather be a master of manifestation? Is it so horrible to accept that you got yourself into this situation and that only you can cultivate or change it?

---

4   *www.braungardt.com/Physics/Quantum%2oNonlocality* (Adapted from the Journal Alexandria)

Would it be such a terrible thing: seizing control of your life and moving it in a positive direction? That is what you want, isn't it? You want to be the best you that you can be. After all, you deserve it. Don't you? Yes, *you* do.

For those of you who have that awful feeling in the pit of your stomach at the mere reading of these words, could it be that you've grown comfortable in your current drama, even if it's sort of crappy? Have you become so used to this ever-present scenario that you keep repeatedly creating it, relationship after relationship? No – that's preposterous. Why would you do such a thing? How could you even if you would? These things just happen . . . don't they?

No, they don't! You have a mighty hand in whatever situation you are in at this very moment (you chose to read this book, right?).

Here's a clue:

**If you always do what you always do,
you always get what you always get.**

If you keep attracting losers and weirdos into your life, it's because you keep inviting them in. If your relationships eventually fall apart, it's because that's all you know how to do. As a personal coach, I find it fascinating that while some women never experience physical abuse, still others have suffered multiple attacks. How can this be? Whether consciously or subconsciously, you are manifesting the kinds of relationships you believe in. Your partner *du jour* is a direct reflection on how you view yourself and what you believe is possible. Scary, isn't it? No one makes you lie, stay, love, shut down, stray, or grow. No one is doing it to you; you are doing it to yourself. It's all you, baby. It's all you.

# $\mathcal{A}$ *side bar:*
## CHANGING THE RULES AS WE GO

I had to write this piece completely by myself because Mordant has such strong negative feelings about infidelity, it would just turn into a slam session, and that's not what I want here. I want to illustrate an important point, and the following material does just that.

I know a woman; I'll call her Missy. Missy is a conglomeration of a number of men and women. But again, let's just go with Missy. Missy is not the spouse who flirts or fantasizes; she is the adulteress. We're going to use her to illustrate an important concept.

Missy is a sharp-witted, gorgeous middle-aged woman. Although a swell gal at heart, Missy has lied to and cheated on pretty much every man she's ever committed to. It's what she knows, and now, it's who she is.

Because she is such a smart cookie, she has managed to justify this most dishonest behavior with trendy excuses.

"My spouse rejects me."

"I love my spouse, but I'm in love with so-and-so."

"I deserve to be happy, don't I?"

"I'm not attracted to my spouse any more."

"I'm crying out for help."

"I never knew it could be like this."

"This one's different."

And just how old does a woman have to be before she gets that it's different every time because she's with a different lover? Duh! And, my personal favorite, (drum roll please):

"We've got a spiritual connection. I can feel it when he's thinking about me."

Right, honey. We'll talk about you more in the Personality Types chapter. You'll find your bit in the Low Integrity Syndrome portion. Spiritual connection, my heinie.

Anyhow, sarcasm to the side, Missy lies because she is convinced if people knew her they wouldn't like her. She has a valid point. She lies and betrays, so yeah, I wouldn't trust her any farther than I could throw her. A self-fulfilling prophecy, to be sure.

She changes her outside persona to fit the person she is speaking with, but on the inside, the wall is impenetrable. No one really knows Missy because she only shows what she thinks they want to see. Wow. How lonely. No wonder she's always searching for something outside of herself to make her feel loved.

But why does Missy cheat with some dishonest schmuck who gets off on infidelity? Because, a good, honest man wouldn't play the destructive game she keeps repeating. A good, honest man wouldn't want to be a part of a lie. And the lying Romeo who advocates adultery? Perhaps he thinks she'll change for him, but it's not likely. More likely, this Fantasy Addict is accustomed to space between himself and those he loves, so this fantasy relationship feels comfortable and safe. When the glitter fades, he will too. They always do.

Since distractions tend to be short lived, Missy is forever searching for something new. As always, she shares things with her lover that she "has never shared with any one else" (She says that every time, so she must be running out of these bits by now). She has, once again, forgotten she always shares herself with the new guy and then feels close to him (for a short period of time). The reality of the situation is that if Missy would just quit lying to everyone, she could feel intimate with anyone she chooses. Instead, she has deluded herself into believing he's "special" when the truth is, she's "special" when she's with him, and "special" has yet to last.

I cannot count how many Missys I have spoken with. I cannot count how many times I predicted what would happen next and was correct. All my Missys think their situation is "unique" when in fact it is "common" and therefore, predictable. Unique is when a person rises above their negative pattern and keeps their integrity.

The really sad part is that Missy has made yet another man responsible for her happiness; *and this is precarious.*

For about five minutes, when things were really scary, Missy agrees that she needs help and considers taking time out for a year or two to spend some time alone (and in therapy). Missy has never experienced being alone without being lonely. Poor thing. A little soul searching without the distraction of a lover could help her become intimate with herself, and thus, maybe some day intimate with a romantic partner. But, one good orgasm with the latest tryst and that idea gets trashed. Okay, maybe that was little advanced for our lover girl.

The very real danger in this imbalanced drama is that Missy has become a woman whose highs are too high and don't last, while the lows are dangerously low and consuming. She is clinically manic, and that's no joke. Remember, no one really knows her, so she's completely alone, even though she has tons of sex and conversation. In her twenties this outrageous negative drama was normal. In her forties, it's getting old; but not to her! Based on results, the same dramatic pattern she created in her youth amuses her to this day. So, the sneaking and lying persist. As a matter of fact, it's getting worse.

It's an addiction, and like all addictions, as time passes, Missy needs a bigger, louder, harder, faster rush to feel satisfied. I'm not sure what exists beyond adultery, but it breaks my heart to think what will happen to her if she doesn't figure this out.

I digress.

Here's my point. There was a time when Missy believed in karma. Karma is an energetic law that basically says that *you get back what you put out*. It says we are defined by our actions, not our words. As Missy was trying to convince me that it was indeed okay to lie to and cheat on her husband, I asked her if she believed in karma any more. Missy did not skip a beat.

"No," was her answer.

"Well, when you were screwing your Yoga teacher you were all about the karma," I wanted to say, but realized in that moment that Missy *rewrites the rules to suit each situation*, so she may be allowed to do what ever she wants.

It doesn't occur to Missy that if the action needs to be lied about, she shouldn't do it, because, in her world, there is no repercussion for the ill action. Yeah, she lives with guilt, but she's used to that by now.

Taoist eyes see the repercussions in the fabric of the Universe, but Missy just thinks her life is a big, passionate roller coaster, which something else controls. You doubt it? Ask her to dump her lover. She'll tell you she couldn't help but fall in love with so-and-so, and now she's powerless. She will not accept that she has asked for every bit of pain and negativity that surrounds her; Missy is a Victim of herself.

Q.  How could such a smart lady choose a life of romantic crime?

A.  Personal accountability and rules are absent.

She's not a bad person; she simply has no ethical structure to function inside of. Accountability and rules create inner structure. Missy rewrites the rules every day. So, like an undisciplined child, she lives in fear, and fearful people are capable of anything. We call this "being in survival." Inner structure is a necessary element to stability. Stability is a basic human need in order to feel safe. Stability is why we get jobs, commit to our children, and live in houses. Even if you have mastered the art of Transmutation and are mindfully creating reality from thought waves, you need a firm structure in both body and mind to avoid misuse of power. That's why the Tao works for so many people; it gives them a structure of rules and ethics to follow. Inside of that structure, there is freedom to function and a perceived element of order.

> ***So know now that we do not get to change the rules to suit our situation.* If you choose to take the structure this book offers to heart, and start taking responsibility for your life and the effects you have on the fabric of the Universe, that's pretty much it. Once you understand Taoist Quantum Manifestation, there's no going back and no feigning ignorance. You will reap the repercussions of your actions. So, keep it clean, folks, keep it clean.**

By the way, for all of you who walk a crooked path like Missy, she is actually a great gal. She's worthy of all the love and joy there is to be had, just like you.

There are two things that separate Missy's experience of intimacy from mine. First, my belief system, or structure, says that there are repercussions for my actions and hers does not. So, when the Universe slaps her in the face with her own behaviors, she just doesn't get it.

Second, I believe that when someone gives me his or her heart, faith, and trust, it is an uncommon and precious gift that should be held with kindness and respect. Based on results, Missy does not believe this. It's her right, but she has no one but herself to blame when her heart and trust get trampled like so much rubbish.

So, in Missy's situation I would have avoided guilt and humiliation by refraining from actions I would have to lie about. Pretty simple, huh? End one relationship before consummating another; even if that means hurting someone's feelings or losing them completely. It would be nice to test one relationship before I let go of my current one, but I am absolutely convinced that a relationship whose foundation is based on lies will propagate unhappiness and more lies. There is no sexual experience, false spiritual awakening, or hormone rush worth the unhappy repercussion betrayal brings.

Missy's path is no more or less holy than mine and I have faith in her, even during times when she does not. I wish she could see that words not only color her presentation, but that a person is also defined by their actions. Perhaps some day she will find a simple belief system based on truth and love and follow it to a place where secrets cannot grow. For now, I have no choice but to trust Missy to be who she is.

## To Continue the Original
## Train of Thought

"But, I *love* this person." A charming thought to be sure. How is it couples start out so inspired to openness and love, but end up shut down, isolated and bitter? Why do people cheat on those they have committed to? Why do couples change when things get real?

The scariest reality of all is that you may be the person behaving poorly in order to spawn a familiar dysfunction. Are you on the receiving end of abusive treatment or did you set it up? The bottom line here is that we are responsible for everything: from the type of people we allow access to our lives, to who we allow ourselves to become in any given situation. If you want anything even vaguely resembling a fabulous romance, it is up to you to seize control and make it so.

> **The notion that others can make us feel good or bad is untrue. Consciously or – more frequently – unconsciously, we are choosing how we feel at every single moment. The external world is in so many ways a mirror of our beliefs and expectations. Why we feel the way we feel is the result of the symphony and harmony of our own molecules of emotion that affect every aspect of our physiology, producing blissful good health or miserable disease.**

–Candace B. Pert, PhD

[5]

We are the authors of our romantic destiny, and it is up to us to write the happy ending.

---

5   *Molecules of Emotion*, page 321 (Candace B. Pert, PhD, Scribner, 1997)

# Hornitos™ Martini

A truly sophisticated way of serving Hornitos™ Añejo - A clear expression of Hornitos™ style.  Sarina prefers hers in an elegant, fine crystal martini glass.

2 parts Hornitos™ Añejo Tequila
1 dash dry Vermouth

Shake ingredients well and pour. Garnish with lime twist, and good friends.

# MYANMAR (FORMERLY BURMA).

I met Anira and her friend Leona at the hotel where I was staying in Mandalay, Myanmar. After hearing that I was researching for this book, they invited me to join them for dinner. While dining that evening I had the privilege of listening to a couple of gals who were most certainly riding the probability waves and shifting into particles of reality most consciously.

"I have been accused of being too Yang," Anira began.

For those of you who aren't familiar with the way of the Tao, Yang means masculine. Yang is the hot, expanding part of nature. The Tai Chi Symbol represents this with its bright or light half. If you look closely, you will see a dark circle in the center of this light side. This is the necessary feminine counterpart, Yin, in the center of all that machismo. Man is Yin wrapped in Yang. That's right ladies; your guy has a soft, chick-flick watching, love-song listening, sensitive person inside of him. Just break their heart once and see how long it takes, if ever, for them to get over it. Most fellas are pretty vulnerable. Why else, other than self-preservation, have so many men mastered the art of shutting down? They shut down because they are too sensitive to handle the intensity of emotions, positive or negative. Remember this when dealing with Yang personalities and treat these folks with extra kindness if you want them to feel safe opening up to you.

Yin is feminine – cool and contracting. Yin is characterized in the Tai Chi symbol as dark with a circle of light in its center. Woman is Yang wrapped in Yin.

Oh, please. You doubt it? How many gals out there are the chief, cook and bottle washer, mother, wife, run their house with an iron fist and work at least part time? This is Yang, my friends. Wrapped up in a pretty package, but Yang nonetheless.

Some of us, at various points in our lives, become imbalanced. Anira and I had something in common. In my youth, I was more masculine than was healthy for a woman. I was reversed and therefore a bit "off." I was incredibly sensitive internally, but never showed it externally. As a young woman, I actually made myself ill more than once from repressing such strong emotions; no one knew.

"I've said, many times," Anira continued, "that I wish I could meet a man more Yang than me. Men seem to crumble at my slightest disapproval. Okay, my disapproval is usually more than slight. Whatever. Point being, it was time to take matters into my own hands, consciously open my heart, and grow the Yin side of my nature with the intention of manifesting a man more Yang than I am."

Leona added, "The question was, was she ready for such trust in the Universe? Was there really a guy out there who wasn't completely inept? Did 'Big Daddy' really exist?"

We all laughed out loud.

Anira went on, "In this endeavor, I was not alone. Leona played a huge part. As she and I spoke of our desire to manifest this experience of extreme Yin and Yang, we unknowingly became like the ladies in the book *The Witches of Eastwick*. The manifesting began the moment we put our minds to it, and with a lot more power behind it than when we practiced on our own. Twice the intention, twice the Chi."

My eyebrows must have risen to my hairline. "You know Chi Kung?" I said.

They both just smiled and nodded as if they held a big secret they could not speak aloud.

"As this Yin in me began to grow, my physical appearance actually started to shift," Anira went on. "My face was softer and my voice was smoother. Men who were truly attracted to Yin women **lost their mind** when I walked by. These fellas appreciated and truly desired a soft, feminine woman. So, romance was in the air as I created myself a Yin female and welcomed Yang men into my space. And enter my space, they did."

Now it was Leona's turn to laugh out loud. "Oh! You should have seen it! This girl was really something."

Anira chimed in. "I had men staring at me in restaurants, following me through town, and I was even kissed by a total stranger. This last macho man could not speak a word of English, but he knew that in the moment we shared, he was the man, I was the woman, and he was calling the shots. He was strong enough to take control, yet *sensitive enough to know where my boundaries were.*"

Anira suddenly had a far away look in her eyes. I know this sounds fantastical, but I swear in that moment of remembrance, the way she looked actually shifted. Her eyes were softer; her face was gentler. It was almost like someone put Vaseline on the camera lens. She just looked softer.

"Anira," I said. "Tell me, in detail, what happened and what you learned. I think this is exactly the sort of story I'm looking for."

She perked right up, ordered martinis for everyone at our table, and started her story.

"Here's how it all went down," said Anira. "On day three of our Myanmar adventure, Leona and I were picked up at 5 A.M. by a horse and buggy to view the sunrise over Bagan. Leona quickly named our trusty steed and driver 'Number 36,' as the driver spoke no English and was driving a carriage with that label. So, by 5:30 A.M. Number 36 had safely delivered us to a tall temple on the edge of an enormous field. At 5:30 A.M. it was black as pitch, but we knew from seeing it the previous day that we were overlooking an area with over 700 stupas and temples, some of which had been there for over 1000 years."

For the newcomer to Myanmar culture, a stupa is a spiritual monument. The stupa represents the Buddha's body, his speech, his mind and every part shows the path to Enlightenment. At the very least, every stupa contains a life tree and a holy relic, so each monument is a national treasure. There was a time when families built these structures for their family to both pray and be remembered by. The wealthier the family, the larger the monument. Rich families built temples through which one may walk inside and climb to the highest levels. Less affluent families built smaller structures to sit outside and pray.

Anira continued. "15 minutes later, Leona and I were five stories up an enormous temple, sitting on a four-foot wide ledge facing the forthcoming sunrise. It was extremely dangerous and tourists would never be allowed on such a dangerous ledge in America."

"Or Europe," said Leona.

"We were looking at nothing," continued Anira, "yet anticipating everything. We had spent the previous day viewing painting after painting of the colorful Myanmar sunrise but somehow thought these artists were exaggerating.

"I should mention that on the way up, our guide had one of those nifty hats with the light on top. I guess we didn't think too much of it then, even though the steps were steep and no more than four or five inches wide. We just followed the light. Once atop, our guide went back to his trusty steed, Number 36, and left us alone – *for about two minutes.*

"You know how when you go to Disneyland or Hollywood Boulevard there's always that group of Asian photographers walking around with cameras hanging from their neck? Well, about 15 of those guys came from nowhere! It was like the crazy clown car at the circus; they just kept coming up the stairs and squeezing themselves onto our ledge. Once atop, Leona and I nearly fell off the edge as they squeezed together and waited for the sunrise by talking loudly and trying to reposition themselves. I was convinced one of them would go careening into the blackness, but they managed to survive regardless.

"Once the sun began to rise, they were clicking cameras wildly and speaking even more. To their credit, they were having a great time, and kudos to them for taking this crazy adventure so they might capture one of the world's most incredible sights. And it *was* an incredible sight. I don't know if I'll ever be able to thank Leona enough for organizing this trip."

She stopped and put a gentle hand on Leona's shoulder. The ladies locked eyes just for a moment. The smile on each face wasn't sexual, but the connection was nearly palpable.

"I do know that there are no words to explain what we witnessed that morning, but I'll try to bring you there with me," said Anira. "Hold on, let's get some *hors d'oeuvres*." And with that she flagged down one of the half dozen waiters at our disposal.

Anira ordered some appetizers and told the wait staff to keep the Martinis coming. As the waiter walked away, Leona gently touched his elbow and asked him to bend down so she could whisper in his ear. When she was done, he smiled at her and said, "Yes ma'am!"

"As the sun begins to rise over Bagan," Anira continued, "the first thing we see is a bluish, silver light which barely illuminates the fine, glowing, gray mist on the ground.

"Everything is some shade of blue. Imagine, we are 5 stories high. At first, we barely see this mist, but then it's like sitting above clouds. The sky turns more definite shades of blue as the sun slowly approaches the skyline.

"The silver clouds beneath us recede as the sun continues to rise, but the effect is that of objects growing upward from the earth. Within minutes, faint suggestions of hundreds of dark blue spires slowly rise from the huge field and transform into solid structures. Soon, you can see the shadows of dark blue temples beneath the spires as they begin to take solid form. Again, everything is a shade of blue, and to this day, I've never seen anything like it."

"There are no modern structures," Leona added. "No electric or phone wires, no streetlights, no modern buildings, no roads leading anywhere, just monuments to the Buddha."

"Within minutes," Anira said, "the sky shifts and pink and orange begin to take over the blue. Astonished, we continue to see these monuments, these stupas, rise from the ground as the mist slowly disappears. And before this mist returns to its home underground for the day, we see it reflect an unbelievable array of color from the now salmon and gold rays of sun. Eventually, over 700 stupas and temples rise from their underground slumber and come to the surface in all of their ancient glory, while simultaneously it's night protector, the mist, sinks to it's resting place in the cool earth below.

"The final scene is a clear, bright, cool morning sky over a dry field that houses ancient gold and brick structures which cover the land as far as the eye can see. We are witness to the same sight as the ancestors who built these monuments 1000 years earlier."

Wow.

"Unfortunately," Leona added, "it wasn't as romantic as it could have been because these photographers were constantly repositioning themselves for better shots. I asked this big guy next to me to move his massive back out of my line of vision. Interesting task since we spoke different languages."

Anira jumped in. "Which he did with a smile. Being European, Leona must have pondered this communication for some time and had considerable discomfort before requesting his removal." Anira said this with a horrible, but funny British accent. "An American would have jumped right in and told that guy to pick a spot and shut the heck up. *Viva la* difference."

More laughter. The waiter returned with our *hors d'oeuvres* and three more martinis. He waited for us to stop speaking before he set the glasses down. Then, he spoke to Anira and I.

"Ladies, your friend has requested Sauza Hornitos™ Añejo Tequila Martinis. Lemon, no olives. Shaken, not stirred." And with that, he gently set a glass in front of each of us. "To us," said Leona and we all clinked glasses and took a sip of the fiery liquid. Simply delicious.

After some silly conversation about European manners versus American (Anira was American and Leona was German, but had spent considerable time in England), we finished our *hors d'oeuvres* and were just warmed enough by the amazing Hornitos™ Martinis to be ready for dinner. We pondered our menus and ordered.

"OK, ladies, when we last left our adventurous gals, you were admiring the Myanmar sunrise," I said.

"Right," Anira said. "When the glitter had faded and the light of day was purely upon us, we prepared to make our descent down the temple and back to Number 36. Leona went first, followed by the large male photographer, then me. Well, it should have been me, but the moment I took two steps down, I developed a sudden and intense fear of walking down super narrow, super steep, super dark steps. So I called down to Leona and told her I didn't think this was gonna work for me. I told her I'd just stay right where I was and make my way down after everyone had left.

"Leona was busy explaining to me that I should turn around and descend like I was on a ladder, when the big photographer guy between us began gesturing oddly. He was patting his left shoulder with his right hand in a move that said 'jump on, honey!' Yeah, right. Ignoring him I said, 'Okay, Leona. I'll do that, but I want to get out of line and go last.'

"Before I knew what happened, this big Asian guy had grabbed my wrists and maneuvered my arms over his shoulders. He then proceeded to lift me on to his back while he was precariously standing on those skinny, steep steps. To my utter amazement, this total stranger just started carrying me down the temple stairs. No matter what I did, how I struggled, or how loud I yelled into his thick neck, this man never wavered; not once. He was a rock who steadily made his way down long, narrow corridors with his load securely fastened to his strong back via his hearty grip.

"Once we had descended three of the four stories, he put me down. Probably sick of the yelling, but secure the crazy American lady could comfortably get herself down one flight of narrow steps. I was so shocked and embarrassed; I took off without seeing his face, much less saying thank you. Leona noticed my rudeness and gently scolded me later."

Leona just smiled. We all took another sip of our martinis and marveled how wonderful straight Hornitos™ tasted. I noticed for the first time that our martinis were in gorgeous crystal glasses. And, in contrast to the Thai whiskey I was accustomed to, I felt lucid and elegant, never losing composure. We were three women, sipping fine liquor from fine crystal, having a wonderful evening. Life was good.

Anira went on.

"Once safely back with old Number 36, I hid until Leona came to join me for the ride home. Of course, we chatted on the morning's bizarre happenings, and we concurred that it was an interesting coincidence. We had been discussing the desire for a masculine man and one just happened to show up this morning. Interesting.

"During the course of the day we reflected further when we were not completely awed by the culture, sights, and sounds of Bagan. Leona bought over a dozen longee."[6]

Leona chimed in, "We each purchased an authentic, hand-made lacquer box, too – after watching the grueling process by which they are created. The boys were absolutely riveted by Anira. So much flirting!"

"All in all, a great day." Anira said.

Finally, dinner came. If I could explain the food, I would. But time has stricken the contents of my meal from my memory. Had it not been for a handy-dandy recorder, the story would have been lost as well. What I do recall is being famished, wolfing down my meal and Hornitos™.

"The next morning we were in the taxi bright and early making our way to the airport," Anira continued.

Sarina's Note: When in Myanmar, you will be told to be at the airport two hours prior to takeoff. This rule is in place because Myanmar flights leave when the plane is available, not when the schedule dictates. This means if your plane is on the runway one hour before it is due to depart, it goes. It may also mean you will sit at the airport for an hour or two after the scheduled departure time with absolutely no announcement. Just thought you may want to know in case you're ever in Myanmar. Now, back to Anira's story.

"So we're in this taxi and Leona blurts out, 'That guy! That man from the temple yesterday! He's going to be at the airport! I just know it!'

"You have to know Leona to know how bizarre that is. She is a sensitive woman, but not one who would advertise her psychic ability."

"What could I do? I had to tell her what I just knew," said Leona with a smile.

Anira went on, "So I said, 'Umm, Leona. You do realize that I will never recognize him. I had my face buried in his neck the whole time we were, uh, together.'

---

6    A longee is the Myanmar version of a sarong worn by most native men and women.

"'I'll recognize him,' she says. 'I'll never forget him. You'll see; he'll be there.'

"Sure enough, once we checked in and were seated in the waiting area, Leona took off. I actually didn't think much of it until she returned with a great big Asian man at her side. You could have knocked me over with a feather. I knew this was my guy from the day before. Leona was beaming. I can't remember if she said anything as I was locked on this guy. All I remember was the look on his face when our eyes met. He was locked on to me in some bizarre energetic connection between strangers."

Anira took a minute and ate some of her dinner. I asked Leona if she wanted to tell some of this story and she politely declined. She said this was really Anira's tale.

After a few more bites, Anira picked up where she had left off. "This total stranger sat down extremely close to me and smiled. I tried to say hello, but we soon discovered he spoke no English and I spoke no Korean. I will withhold the name of the association he was connected to, to protect his identity, but suffice to say I learned he was Korean and that he was with a group of artists. I don't know what came over me, but this stranger suddenly became the focal point of my world. Everything else turned to mist and it was just we two.

"The language barrier prohibited conversation, so in an effort to express my gratitude for carrying me down the stairs, I flexed my biceps and pointed at him while saying, 'You are a very strong man.' He totally 'got it' and proceeded to demonstrate his prowess by opening his coat slightly to expose his massive chest covered with a snug sweater. He then flexed his pectoral muscles in a rapid staccato. Normally, I would have laughed or been offended, but in an odd turn of emotion, I was utterly charmed by the rawness of his masculinity. After displaying his manly chest he raised his muscular leg, lifted the hem of his pants a couple of inches, and revealed his powerful calf muscle. Again, I was charmed. What a guy.

"Before I could think to do anything else, he jumped up and ran over to his travel bag. When he returned, he had gifts for Leona and I. Korean liqueur – Leona's came in a handy-dandy box – and cigarettes. He opened the cigarettes and pulled one part way out to show me how thin and lovely they were. You remember; those skinny cigarettes from the 80's that were popular for about five minutes? Anyway, he was very proud to present us with these gifts, and we were delighted to accept them. Leona thought it was very European of him to give gifts to the lady and her chaperone.

"He pulled out his camera and took a gorgeous photo of Leona. He was really something. Then he took a photo or two of me. I was invited to view the photos on his digital camera after he had showed them to Leona.

"As I put my face close to his to view the small screen on his camera, I noticed right away that this was by far the most natural – I had no make-up on – awesomely beautiful photo taken of me in months. This stranger had captured the Yin I had been trying to cultivate. I was blown away at the gentleness and openness portrayed in these photos. Was this how he saw me?

"I saw a few other shots, some of which were of the Myanmar splendor and were of professional quality. When I looked up, he was staring at me. Our faces were maybe six inches apart. Now, this man was no fashion model, but in that moment he was the most beautiful, masculine man I had ever seen. I know it sounds crazy, but like my friend Emo says: 'Our eyes met. Our lips touched. And we just knew.' It was unbelievable. I let a total stranger gently kiss me and leave. I felt faint as I watched him walk out of the terminal and board his plane.

"When I could move, I turned around to find Leona. She was leaning against a wall, watching with tears streaming down her beautiful face. We both felt like the world had stopped for a moment and were walking in a different dimension. How did she know? Why was she so compelled to search the airport until she found this man for me? We were in awe and yet, simultaneously we knew we had been the co-creators of this bizarre encounter. As I said, we were like the *Witches Of Eastwick*; we put our energies together and manifested a man who was macho enough to be more Yang than me while being sensitive enough to feel my boundaries. Wow.

"Well, 30 minutes later, we were in an airplane headed for Mandalay. We had to go there because they wrote that song about the road that leads to this mysterious place. Of course, we were blabbering about our unbelievable experience for the entire 40-minute ride."

"Wait a minute!" I said. "We're in Mandalay right now. This just happened in the last few days?"

Leona and Anira smiled and nodded. Then Anira continued.

"Once in Mandalay, we met our guide for the day and proceeded to the taxi. We were still at the airport just waiting to be driven to a place where Leona could purchase a Myanmar nun's outfit when we started talking about the whole Korean guy thing again. We sat in the car and marveled at how powerful we were to have manifested this macho man. We marveled at how swept away he must have been to publicly display affection for a total stranger in front of his companions.

"As we were speaking in the back seat, Leona's gaze moved past me and out the side window. Her jaw dropped and she caught her breath.

"'You're not going to believe this. Look outside,' she said. I turned my head and looked to my left. Outside, standing on the sidewalk, just outside my taxi door was the Korean man. He was looking right at me. This man must have taken a charter flight to Mandalay with his group. I saw a van filled with his companions, all of whom were watching out the windows. He must have seen me come out of the airport and enter the taxi. This guy just got out of the van, walked across the traffic, and stood outside my door. He waited for me to initiate contact by allowing me to be the one to open the door.

"After a moment of shock, I did open my door and said, 'Hello.'

"Once the invitation had been issued, this man – whom I now call my Korean Lion – knelt down so our faces were level with each other. There could be no words. So he gently put an arm around my waist and leaned in to kiss me. This time the kiss was passionate and filled with desire. Unbeknownst to him, this was also the first kiss I had received since parting with my last boyfriend over a year earlier. This kiss was so perfect that when he moved away, I pulled him back for another. His lips were full and soft. His touch was perfect. I am convinced to this day that if we had been alone, I would have returned to the States with a Korean child in my belly. But, as luck would have it, we were in public and only inches away from Leona! Eventually, he stood up, kissed the back of my hand delicately, and walked back a few feet to the curb. I closed the door. He was still standing there, watching me, a moment later when the taxi pulled away."

You could have heard a pin drop at our table. We were all riveted, pensive, a little drunk, and very full. It must have been a whole minute before Anira spoke again.

"Here's the interesting thing. In the presence my Korean Lion, my Yin Chi sparked chivalry and a take-charge attitude. He was as Yang as I was Yin. This macho man knew that before completely ravishing a woman, he must win her and her friends over with good manners and a firm knowledge of polite etiquette. In the absence of flowers and chocolates, he gave my girlfriend and I Korean whisky and cigarettes. That's all he had in his travel bag, and we were delighted at the gesture. It was really something for me to be so well taken care of by this beautiful stranger and just be a woman.

"The Korean Lion simply accepts the fact the he is the man and I am his necessary opposite. He clearly shows a sense of respect and responsibility in the presence of women. I love who I was in his presence and I love how he saw me. He is a Yang male and I, just for a brief time, bathed in the Yin it inspired in me."

Silence for a moment. Then . . .

"Wait a minute," I blurted out, most unprofessionally. "What happened to him? Will you ever see him again? What if he is the love of your life? I mean, he could still be right here, in Mandalay!"

And with that, we all turned toward the door.

I haven't heard from or seen Anira since that night. I have, however, kept in touch with Leona, now back in Germany, and she tells me that her friend retained the powerful Yin Chi for a few months when she returned to the States. She is currently a bit more Yang, but says she will never be the same as she may draw upon this gentle power at will now and continues her quest for balance.

I hope she sees this book and reads this excerpt, and that it reminds her of how powerful, feminine and beautiful she is.

# Hornitos™ Mexican Sunrise

## OR

## The Way Without Force

The Hornitos™ take on a tequila classic; bursting with fruit which is balanced with the natural expression of pure agave flavor found in Hornitos™ Plata.

2 parts Hornitos™ Plata Tequila
Juice from one freshly squeezed orange
Juice from one freshly squeezed lime
2 parts pineapple

Fill a drink shaker with all the ingredients, shake and strain into a glass. Garnish with an orange and lemon wheel.

# Chapter 2

## DEFINITION OF THE TAO

The Way of nature.
The Way without force.

**The Way.**

Choice is what the Tao is all about. Choice is what this book is all about. As practitioners and teachers of Taoist meditation, Mordant and I have found a concrete and real way to ferret out excess negative emotions and transform them into positive vitality. Not only do we teach meditation, we do it. That's right. I said we meditate. We, and thousands of others who practice meditation, have finally figured out *how to pick another way to be.*

Here's the deal. Life can be rich and full of beauty or life can be frightening and bitter, as well as a plethora of realities in between. It is important to acknowledge that each one of us is ultimately responsible for our own experience. Meditation can help ease the burden of that responsibility. Quiet the racket in your mind and maybe, just maybe, you can hear yourself.

Try to follow me here. One of the biggest reasons people are so tweaky in intimate relationships is because of emotional imbalances; i.e. too much fear, anger, worry, anxiety, sadness, depression, hatred, cruelty, hastiness, and impatience to name a few. This is not to say we want to be imbalanced in the other direction, either. Even too much joy is still *too much.*

When we are emotionally *im*balanced, the things we believe in and thus manifest are reflections of that imbalance. Conversely, a state of emotional balance allows us to see, clearly, the limitless healthy choices before us. Emotional balance propagates feelings of compassion, respect, and gratitude. People who aspire to a state of emotional balance quickly tire of painful relationships that ultimately stand between them and a life of joyful celebration. Certain meditative practices bring about a state of emotional balance.

As stated clearly in chapter 1, another huge reason people ruin relationships is because they have no structured belief system. Remember, without structure, we are like children who are insensitive to the repercussions of our actions. If you don't understand that your actions matter, you become open to lying, cheating, stealing, and other abusive behaviors; you are floundering in survival. So, finding a healthy belief system and experiencing the freedom of commitment is beneficial if you want to stay in a healthy relationship.

I'm going to take a quantum leap of faith here, and suggest that every single one of you go online and find your local Universal Healing Tao instructor. Take a class on the Inner Smile and Six Healing Sounds. It's easy and gets straight to the point.

There aren't a lot of us, but the few that exist are listed on www. UniversalTao.com. This book is not about how to meditate, but I would be remiss if I acted like I was just born happy, balanced, and enlightened.

Okay, maybe I was, but I certainly lost site of that by the time I started dating. I was unhappy, unsatisfied, dishonest, and victimized by the time I was 17. I found my way out by sticking to my program and applying some simple techniques, which ultimately put me in a position to pick another way to be. Today, I am aware that each relationship and every experience I perceive is the result of whom I choose to be in that moment. My actions do matter to others and I allow those I trust to affect me as well.

Lastly, Mordant asked me to explain the Tao on the onset of this book so those of you new to this concept could understand a little Eastern Philosophy. To that I refer to the immortal words of Laozi:

**The Tao that can be *told* is not the eternal Tao.**
**The Tao that can be *named* is not the eternal Tao.**

If you want to study Taoism, read the *Tao Te Ching*. I highly recommend it. Still, others enjoy the *Tao of Pooh* and the *Te of Piglet*. There is a chapter in this book solely dedicated to meditations and mantras for healthy dating; check it out.

If you are new to philosophy and have no interest in meditation, you may still read and understand this text. There may be a few concepts that float over your head, but digest this information with your mind, eyes, and heart. You'll absorb what you were meant to.

**This is the Tao.**
**The Way of nature.**
**The Way without force.**
**The Way.**

Throughout this book are short stories illustrating the numerous points of the Tao of Intimacy and practical applications of Taoist Quantum Manifestation.

There is a firm reason I am sharing the following story. It illustrates "picking another way to be," the power of choice and the detriment one functions under without it.

## ANOTHER WAY TO BE (OR NOT TO BE)

When Trixie was in her early twenties, a relative noticed a bizarre phenomenon at the grocery store. She was shopping with her Aunt Abbey one day, and Aunt Abbey blurted, "God, Trix, you could wear a bag over your head and every creepy guy in the store would still follow you." It may have been the fabulous hooker attire, but Abbey suspected it was something deeper which compelled the unsavory fellows to follow Trixie around the store.

When they arrived back home, Aunt Abbey said, "Aren't you going to the bar with your friends tonight?" Trixie was.

Aunt Abbey said, "Are you interested having a different experience tonight? Are you interested in NOT attracting the creepy guys?"

*Sure*, thought Trixie. *Like that'll happen*. But when she opened her mouth, "Uh, yeah. Sure. Why not?" came out.

"Okay, then. Tell me, who are you when you go to the bar?"

"What do you mean?" Trixie said.

"Well, what do you do at the bar? How do you behave around men?"

Trixie thought about it for a moment and replied, "I usually find a fellow I think is attractive and sort of hone in on him. I make an effort to establish eye contact. If he looks at me, I give him a little smile. If he smiles back, I'm 'in.' Then, I just sit back and let him think it was all his idea."

"And how do you dress?"

"Sexy."

"Would it be accurate to say that when you go to the bar with your friends, who you are is *sexy*?"

"Yes."

"Okay. Now, I want you to *pick another way to be*. Anything but sexy."

Trixie was stumped. She actually could not fathom another way, other than sexy, to be. She thought, *Why go out if we're not looking for guys? And what better way to attract guys than with sex?*

Trixie had no answer for Abbey. So, Aunt Abbey called in re-enforcements. She called her husband into the room. "Scott, Trixie here is going to the bar with her friends tonight. She has to pick a way to be that is not sexy. Any ideas?"

' Silly," he said.

' Silly it is. Thanks, honey."

'Alright, Trix. Tonight the persona is silly," Aunt Abbey said boldly with a huge smile.

That night Trixie entered the family room in a black dress that showed no cleavage. It came neatly to the knee and she donned matching black pumps. Everyone thought she looked like a real lady. Then, she showed them her secret weapon.

"I have decided that tonight, if I spy an attractive man, I will put these on to avoid trouble. Silly enough?" Trixie produced a small pair of tanning bed goggles from her front pocket and placed them on her nose. Everyone laughed.

And here's what happened next . . .

Underneath the conservative, long black dress was a mini-skirt and a tight, low-cut shirt. Trixie ended up drinking so much beer that night that she made herself ill, passed out in her car (in the dead of winter), and almost froze to death.

Aside from learning that wearing Florida attire during winter in Wisconsin is bad, when Trixie awoke, she became aware that Aunt Abbey's advice was so confronting that she sort of lost her mind and went violently the other way. She saw clearly that she was not committed to this new paradigm of thought. Rather, she was committed to staying with what she knew; and what she knew was hurting her.

For Trixie, this was the beginning of a new life. The importance of being able to "pick another way to be" became the foundation of her quest for balance and freedom. Although she continued to act out her insane need for attention in very unattractive ways for a few years after this incident, this was a turning point for Trixie. She likened it to the apple in the Garden of Eden. Once the knowledge was imparted, she had no choice but to acknowledge that she was creating situations based on her mental state, personal needs, and beliefs. She knew each time she manifested romantic negativity, she had chosen an unhealthy way to be.

Today, Trixie is married to a wonderful man. When asked how she did it, she says, "I choose to be happy."

# Hornitos™ Traditional Margarita

OR

## The Classy Gal's Answer to Whiners & Complainers

A favorite classic, the Hornitos™ Traditional Margarita is a great way to enjoy the smooth taste and tequila edge that Hornitos™ is known for.

1 part Hornitos™ Reposado Tequila
3/4 part Triple Sec Liqueur
1 part sweet & sour mix

Rim the outside of a margarita glass with lime and dip into salt. Add ice to the glass.

Fill a drink shaker with ice, add all ingredients and shake well. Strain the mixture into the glass and garnish with a lime wedge.

# Chapter 3

# PERSONALITY TYPES

The following is a short list of personality types of which you should be aware. When this chapter began, in 1995, it was my ode to how awful men were. Upon re-inspection, Mordant found some gems in the sarcastic diatribe, and the whole thing was painstakingly re-vamped. He found that each gender shares both creepy behavior and an attraction to creepy behavior. He found that even good people behave poorly and that those same people may transform their negativity simply by being aware of it and having the desire to be healthier people.

So, dear reader, resurrected from the dead . . .

~~Personality Types Worthy of Loathing~~
## Personality Types Worthy of Acknowledging

As I've stated previously in this text, you invite people into your life daily; each and every one a unique consciousness behind the human eyes. Your family, your best buddy, even the strangers seated next to you at the café could impact you if you let them. Like a stream, for example, when certain boulders appear, there is opportunity to change direction or perhaps to just have a splash. Once you know who you are, who you attract, and who you are attracted to, it's up to you to decide what, if anything, happens next.

I asked Mordant to go over these for me and thus you will see the term "us" as we speak to you here. I needed a guy's perspective, and he just happens to have one. He's also funny as hell.

The following pages offer a glimpse into a few of the personality types you may encounter – both in others and in yourself. In keeping with the structure of this book, I have interspersed a relevant short story with the drier text.

## THE VICTIM

> **In the presence of a Victim, you will ultimately become the Persecutor. If you hang out long enough, it is inevitable.**
>
> **-Sarina Stone**

> **Failure is an opportunity. If you blame someone else, there is no end to the blame. Therefore the Master fulfills her own obligations and corrects her own mistakes. She does what she needs to do and demands nothing of others.**
>
> **-Laozi**

## VICTIM (vik-tim)[1]

➤ a person or thing made to suffer by a cause which is stated or implied
➤ a living creature offered up as a sacrifice
➤ someone who is cheated or made a dupe

Victims are easily recognizable because they are (a) unhappy and (b) their unhappiness is *never* the result of their own doings. They honestly believe that they are life's Victim. Everything they see and hear is viewed from that perspective. Victim glasses tend to be glued on very tightly.

Unfortunately, since manifestation on the physical plane begins in the realm of the mind, these people really are as screwed as they think they are and there's not a thing you can do about it. Trust us, we've tried. Often they will construe your loving advice as judgmental and closed-minded, thus turning you into a Persecutor. You know how impossible it is to change someone, so the only thing

---

1 The New Lexicon Webster's Dictionary of the English Language 1988 Lexion Publications Inc. page 1096

you can really do is back off and let 'em hate life. Of course, your lack of support will throw them into an episode of negative thinking that ultimately leads them to even more pain. It's lose-lose here.

The true Victim does not want the responsibility that comes with seizing control of life. They would rather sit back, relax, and allow life to happen to them. This way they never have to bear the responsibility of being the captain of their own ship. If things are out of control, and they usually are, then it must be somebody else's fault. Probably the one who's closest to them. If you're dating a Victim, that would be you. Perhaps the most entertaining quality of our lovable Victim types is their charming capacity for directing their emotional arsenal at your face and blowing it off when you least expect it.

Your gut instinct may be to willingly jump into the clutches of this manipulative monster and engage in a pointless struggle, or worse, try to make them feel better. The only way to avoid this catastrophe is to summon up all of your strength and walk away, feeling as though you have left your crying child at school for the first time. Television has glorified Victims. The church has taught us martyrs are good. People who think it's appropriate to save Victims surround you.

But we know better.

## Why are you attracted to Victims?

This means that if you date a Victim, you are comfortable with Victims on some level. You want Victims. You love Victims. Perhaps they make you feel superior. Perhaps you're a "Fixer." Perhaps looking in the mirror and seeing the reflection of the Victim aspect of you is an unconscious comfort zone. Only you may determine why you are attracted to Victims, and only you can change the condition of addiction that forces you to seek out this personality type.

Sometimes Victims are family members or loved ones that you don't wish to write off because you sincerely care for them. There's too much history there and you're not willing to create a life without them. If this is the situation, ask yourself, "Does this person add value to my life?" If they do, weigh out the positives and the negatives. If the positives outweigh the negatives, you must accept that wacky personality quirks are not personal. Detach yourself and accept their gifts with unconditional love.

If the negatives outweigh the positives, our condolences. We understand and we feel for you. Really we do. Keep working on yourself, imaging a better life as you go. Do not become attached to their outcome, only yours.

Another reason for being attracted to Victims is that they are great fixer-uppers. If you are a "Fixer," consider that it is not love which has bound you to the Victim. Lack of desire to seize control of your own life has kept you involved. You spend so much time solving your partner's problems that you never have time to look at your own. You will always have something to do and will always be able to avoid yourself in the chaotic presence of a Victim.

There is a sense of detachment that comes with working on another person's problems. Dealing with their drama is not as invasive as dealing with your own. You're not as emotionally involved, so the answers come easier. In fact, you are probably quite brilliant when it comes to giving advice to the Victim. If they would only follow through and do what you tell them to, they'd be just fine. You're a good person who is helping another person with your wisdom and advice. Of course, the Victim cannot take your advice if it is healthy, that would negate the condition of Victimization in which they live. So, if you do it just right, you always have something to do that takes time away from dealing with your own issues! Yay!

Lastly, the most horrifying reason for dating a Victim is that you like having the Victim around because a Victim feeds your need for superiority and being right. It happens. Is it happening to you?

## But seriously folks . . .

Like an alcoholic, you cannot help a Victim. The Victim must help themself. If you try to save one, rest assured they'll latch on and try to pull you down with them.

Remember, it's common to be frustrated with a Victim and thus become exactly what they want you to be: a Persecutor. Speaking of Persecutors, it's time to meet our next Personality Type . . .

# THE PERSECUTOR

**In the presence of a Persecutor, you will ultimately become their Victim. If you hang out long enough, it is inevitable.**

**-Sarina Stone**

**PERSECUTE (per'se-kut)**
➢ to cause to suffer especially for religious or political reasons
➢ to vex, harass[2]

## Making you wrong is the first goal of a Persecutor.

Know now, in the presence of a Persecutor you will ultimately become their Victim. If you hang out with them long enough, it is inevitable. Persecutors are easily recognizable because (a) they will clearly illustrate your shortcomings and (b) create shortcomings for you if you are lacking.

## Superiority is the second goal of a Persecutor.

The Persecutor gets a short-term buzz when Chi is given to them via psychological or physical bullying. You know, some people get a buzz from walking on the beach. Still others feel energized by laughing children. Then, there are those who get their jollies from humiliating and degrading the people they say they love. We all tend to extract energy from different situations, but Persecutors get theirs by belittling those around them, so they create arena's of communication where they have imagined scenarios of superiority. Ultimately, when they get to know you, a hard core Persecutor may replace love and support with contempt and annoyance.

A Persecutor will question your decisions, point out how you inconvenience them, and tend to harp. When they get on a roll, there's just no way out. It's kind of like playing tennis with one of those automatic ball-throwing machines. If you don't shut them down, they'll keep pitching.

Watch for conversations that start with "What the heck are you talking about?" Or "I can't believe you're honestly considering. . . ." We've all seen it. That couple who comes to the party and looks so normal. Then, one scolds the other for something inconsequential

---

2    The New Lexicon Webster's Dictionary of the English Language 1988 Lexion Publications Inc. page 748

and openly shows an attitude of irritation or flat out contempt in an effort to publicly belittle their partner. Persecutor attitudes are not gender specific and are irritating no matter who the jackass is.

# Why-oh-why would anyone want to be matched with a Persecutor?

The brutal reality is that no one healthy would. A healthy person does not prefer to keep company with someone who constantly points out their faults, or worse yet, attempts to keep them in an inferior position by belittling them. If you find this to be the theme of your relationships, the question is not what is wrong with these people; the real question is what is the matter with you? Make no mistake, allowing yourself continued exposure to this type of treatment is a well-disguised form of self-abuse.

Sarina always says that Victims and Persecutors have to date each other; no one else will have them. So, watch your inner Victim if you keep dating Persecutors.

Mordant says a benefit of dating a Persecutor is freedom from responsibility. One may hide in the shadow of a Persecutor quite easily. After all, you're an idiot, aren't you? Why bother trying when it is so frickin' obvious that you can't take care of yourself? Thank you, Mr. and Ms. Persecutor for making it so easy to take a backseat to life.

## But seriously folks . . .

Victims and Persecutors are very similar. The main difference between the two is that the Victim will try to guilt you into doing or feeling something and the Persecutor will try to bully you.

## What shall I do, you ask?

It is impossible to be intimate with a Persecutor, so don't bother trying to please one in hopes they will love you.

Instead, adopt a healthy sense of humor. Give them what they deserve and smack them in the mouth with it. Not literally – figuratively. (Although we do understand the temptation.) This means if the conversation begins with "You're not really going to wear that, are you?" your answer should be something along the lines of "You know I live to please you, sweetheart. Do you suppose you could teach a class on this fascinating subject? In the mean time, I guess I'll just have to be content with being tasteless lil' old me." OR, for those with a flair for the dramatic, try this one on for size: "What! You don't like my outfit!? I'm doomed. I can't go on!" Flinging your hand up to your forehead and sighing heavily would accentuate this moment. If your beloved Persecutor has any sense of humor, they just might see how creepy they are behaving and snap out of it. At the very least, you prove to yourself that you won't sit there while someone speaks down to you.

Of course, there's always the old stand-by of simply speaking your truth. Tell this person that they do not have permission to speak to you with disrespect and ask them to adopt a more polite attitude. Sometimes being up front breaks the cycle of verbal abuse. Sometimes the Persecutor is just looking for an equal who won't let them get away with it and thus build respect and equality.

Remember, you always have the freedom to take action. Not action for or against your partner, but action within yourself. A common misconception is that you can transform another person into your own immaculate conception of Romeo or Juliet. This is about as effective as gluing the wings back on a butterfly after it has hit the grill of a speeding car. Not only is it ineffective, but you run a serious risk of becoming a horrible monster we call the dreaded Control Freak.

## Why Real Women Drink Straight Tequila
## –Part One–

The coffee smelled wonderful. It was early morning in Chiang Mai, Thailand, and we were sitting in a funky coffee shop called The Sawatdee Cup. Unconsciously, I inhaled deeply. What was I thinking last night? I vaguely remember watching a Thai Kickboxing match and professing my undying love to a Thai fighter named Ass. I don't know if that's how he spelled it, but that was how it was pronounced. While traveling Asia, I have met women named Ma'am, Mint, Gift, and Nit, and once a man named No, but the Kickboxing Ass definitely won the prize for wacky names.

Mordant shot me an inquiring look. Could he tell I was in pain? This morning I chose to have a hangover, because last night I chose to drink Thai whiskey with some outrageous Irish tourists. Thai whiskey will do that to you. In a perfect world, I would only drink Sauza Hornitos™. But Chiang Mai is only perfect to those of us who

37

appreciate life's imperfections, so watered down Thai whiskey and open air kickboxing seemed perfect; until I woke up this morning. Ugh.

"Partying with the boys last night? How's your head?" he asks, the smirk playing across his features. I chose to ignore it. The hangover was taking up too much of my headspace, and I wasn't in the mood for clever.

As I set down my cup to speak, one of the four waiters hovering nearby rushed over to ask if I needed anything else. I smiled politely and told him no. Watching him scurry back, I shook my head at no one in particular. I knew that if I had told him yes, he would have replaced my old cup with a new. This one also filled to the brim with eye-popping, gut-wrenching instant coffee.

I have traveled all over the world, and have yet to see any so attentive as the Thai and Myanmar wait staff. It is a bit unnerving and at times makes private conversation nearly impossible. Today, the customer/waiter ratio was almost equal, and not for a lack of patronage. Looking around, I saw that the other clientele had their own waiters to contend with. This overabundance of wait staff is the Thai way, and it's really quite charming once you get used to all the swooping and pouring.

I opened my mouth to speak a second time, but stopped myself short. The conversation at the next table had suddenly become both loud enough to hear and interesting enough to listen to. I held a finger to my lips to forestall any further comment from the one-man peanut gallery, and we both listened as the scene played itself out. Mordant, being an incurable romantic and a student of the Tao, and I, being both Jewish and female, became transfixed and ultimately involved . . .

"Look, Marcus, all I'm saying is that since we've been here it feels like we're growing apart. We don't talk like we used to. We don't laugh at the same things anymore. At times, it doesn't even feel like we're in the same room. This trip was supposed to bring us together. It's not working, and you seem too distracted to notice."

The distraught woman fidgeted with her empty coffee cup as the silence stretched out between them. Noise from the busy café filled the lonesome space with the sound of clinking china and more social patrons. The uncomfortable quiet continued to draw out between them until tears spilled down the woman's cheeks.

The high-pitched staccato of a passing scooter blared sharply, startling the already tense woman and rousing her from quieter thoughts. "Are you even listening to me?" she said sadly.

Marcus, who had been looking off at nothing in particular, slowly turned to stare blankly at the woman. He said nothing, a dull gaze still lingering on his face like a wall. This appeared to steel the woman's resolve. She continued her contention before the threat of a second silence could manifest into another symphony of cups, saucers, and background noise. "You have no problem going off on your own and exploring without me. And, frankly, I don't mind the time alone." Then she looked him square in the eye and said, "I find myself looking at other men."

Marcus made the mistake of continuing to stare blankly. "And, honey, believe me – they're looking back," she said with a sneer.

"All this and a wandering eye, too," said Marcus dryly.

## Sarina's Observation:

How boring. In about two minutes she went from, "Gee honey, I feel like we're growing apart," to "Gee honey, there sure are a lot of hot guys around here." That's the oldest game in the book. How about trying something new and original? And, like a young, inexperienced man would, he completely forgot everything else she said the moment she insinuated she was interested in other men. How predictable!

She became manipulative when she thought he was ignoring her. But, this guy wasn't ignoring her, he was thinking. There's a difference. Sometimes when a man doesn't know what to say, he says nothing. That's actually the mark of a wise sage. Too bad our girl projects rejection instead of wisdom onto her guy and his silence.

On a second note, ladies, take a lesson from a gal who's been around the block more than once. The "make 'em jealous" routine is a bad idea. Sometimes it works for a short time, but ultimately your man will figure out that you are not to be trusted. I know women who play that game and believe me, it only works on men with low self-esteem. And we know how much fun those guys are. [See Low Self-Esteem in the Personality Types section.]

Be a lady. Be a woman. Stick to the subject at hand and don't distract your man with silly reasons to be jealous. Aside from creating needless negative drama, you show your man that when the going gets tough, you get slutty.

## Mordant's Observation:

I thought Marcus's girlfriend was doing well at first. She was open and loving. She tried talking to him, clearly and concisely naming the issue and conveying that it bothers her. "It feels like we're growing apart." It seems clear to me. However, with Marcus pretending not to listen, she lost her healthy structure almost immediately. This young lady is reactive. She's in pain, obviously afraid, and feeling vulnerable. I think she feels the need to protect herself. So, she's becoming a bit of a Control Freak. On top of that, this girl is fishing for the one thing she really wants from her lover: contact. Even if that contact is negative.

Marcus is not helping matters with the macho soundproof wall, so I'm not feeling quite as empathetic toward him as Sarina is right now. He needs to take responsibility for the message he is projecting. Making a show of not listening was a big mistake and frankly, in my opinion, rude. Not a good sign from an intimate partner.

So, when the open truth did not work, she moved on to another tactic. Jealousy. Marcus was ignoring her, so she felt abandoned. In her mind, Marcus had deserted her and this strange and wondrous place called Thailand had become a lonely prison. This tactic was certainly working. I'm a guy. I know. Marcus had taken the bait and wiped the uncaring glaze from his eyes faster than she could say "other men." She had Marcus's attention now, and that's exactly what she wanted . . .

"My wandering eye? Who talks like that?"

"Now you're just being a bitch."

"Well, I wasn't like this before! Marcus, when we first got together, you were so wonderful. I never wondered what you were thinking. It was like you were an open book to me. Come on Marcus, it's me, Miranda."

Miranda wiped fresh tears from her eyes with an already soaked napkin. Her face was flush with emotion as more tears spilled down her now red cheeks.

Finally, Marcus spoke. "Look, I don't know what you want me to say. I'm trying to figure things out, too, and it would really help if you didn't attack me right now. Honey, I know it looks bad. I just need a little space to work some things out. I know you can't help but take it personally, but really, it's mostly just me."

Miranda glared at him. "Well, you'd better figure yourself out soon. I'm getting tired of being strung along like this. I want a boyfriend. If you're not interested anymore, just say the word! I'm a big girl, Marcus. I can take it. Besides, I'm sure that I'll have no problem finding someone who's not confused and who actually wants my company."

"I just asked you to back off and two seconds later you're attacking me again. Give me a break! Damn it!" Silence for a moment, and then he spoke again. "You're a real piece of work, Miranda. I can't imagine why I'd rather process my personal shit without you."

Miranda's stopped short, her mouth hanging open. Ignoring Marcus's barb, she went on. "You used to tell me you loved me all the time. Now you almost never say it. Mostly, I just feel ugly and in the way."

An untimely waiter, doing his job with perfect precision, ignored the tension at the table and chose that moment to interrupt. "More coffee?" he asked in lightly accented English. He had been dealing with tourists all his life.

"N-no. No thank you," Miranda stammered. She was having trouble focusing, and the thought of more instant coffee sounded anything but appetizing. Without further interaction, the waiter removed her cup, leaving Miranda empty-handed. Still fidgeting from an excess of nervous energy, she settled for picking at her fingernails.

"And I suppose your low self-esteem is my fault, too." Marcus had brought the conversation right back to its pre-interruption low.

"This isn't about my self-esteem," Miranda hissed.

"Like hell it isn't. Look, we're on top of each other 24/7 out here. The first time I tried to create a small gap of "me" space, you became clingy and neurotic. And every day since then, it's just gotten worse. I can't breathe around you."

"What the hell are you talking about?" Miranda shrieked through her tears. "We're supposed to be on vacation together, you jackass."

"I'm talking about you acting like we're glued at the hip. Haven't you been listening to a thing I've said?"

41

"I'm listening, but you're not making any sense."

"I'm making perfect sense. I probably should have talked to you about this earlier, but I didn't know what to say. I just can't handle who you've become. It seems like you want to handcuff us together. It's been non-stop since we arrived."

"That's a crock, and you know it."

"Really?" Marcus just stared at her again, leaving the accusing question hanging in the air.

"What am I supposed to think? It's obvious by the way you act that you don't want my company any more"

"Are your ears working today?" Just for a moment, he seemed dumbfounded. He paused, then, "Whatever. It's always about you, isn't it, Miranda? I tell you how I feel and all you can do is stress on how that affects you. Great friend, Miranda, really." And with that he began to turn as red as she was.

"It's just that I can see that you'd rather run around Chiang Mai without me. You don't include me anymore. I feel like I'm traveling Asia with a total stranger. What did I really do to turn you off so suddenly? There had to be something. I can't believe you just woke up one day and said "Gee. My girlfriend sucks."

"I just told you what's wrong, and you're doing it right now. Maybe I should write this down for you so you can read it when you're sane."

"Dammit, Marcus! I'm just trying to understand what the hell is going on."

## Sarina's Observation:

Miranda, I don't even know you and you're turning me off. It always amazes me when women think that creating unnecessary pain and misery will somehow bring a couple closer together. Like being a whiny wimp is suddenly a fashionable aphrodisiac. The only thing that shocks me more is when it actually works. Some guys love that crap. Apparently, Marcus is not one of those guys. What ever happened to roping in your guy with mystery and sex? The old stand-bys still work, you know. I don't know to whom Miranda is speaking here, but it isn't Marcus. He says "day," she hears "night." He says "black," she hears "You're in my way you obnoxious, ugly pain in the ass." *Girlfriend*!

## Mordant's Observation:

Miranda's right, though. There is something going on. Again, I'm a guy; I know. One thing is for sure . . . she is never going to figure it out this way. She begins by asking what the problem is, but then quickly opts for an attack the moment her query meets with resistance. First, she questions, and then she kicks. Ouch.

If there was any way that she could detach herself emotionally, enough to look beyond Marcus's taunts, she might be able to hear what the real problem is. She might even be sensitive enough to catch glimpses of what's behind his wall. Marcus says he is suffering from too much face time and needs some space to regroup. Period. Baiting him and throwing leading barbs will only enflame the symptoms while leaving the root issue buried safely away.

"Miranda, I've tried explaining things to you. I've just spent the last few minutes telling you what's going on, and you still don't get it. Are you retarded or something? You haven't heard a thing I've said since we sat down." Marcus checked his watch. "I'm not in the mood for a big fight right now, so I'm going to leave. We'll try again later."

With that, he got up from the table, throwing his napkin down. He quickly pulled out his wallet and tossed enough money to pay the bill.

"I don't need your damned money, Marcus!"

"Whatever, Miranda," Marcus said. He then stuffed his wallet back in its pocket and hurriedly exited the scene, stage right.

Not for the first time this morning, Miranda sat there slack-jawed with tears streaming down her face.

## Sarina's Observation:

I don't even know where to begin. On the one hand, I want to shake Miranda for being so impossible. On the other hand, I want to give this girl great big bear hug because she is so deep into her pain she can't even see that her boyfriend is trying to reach out to her.

There are times in our lives when we regress. A loved one pushed us away when we were five, so at 35 we're still dating people who are emotionally unavailable to re-create this reality. Yeah, that's Psych 101. Will dating these people repair the pain of the past? Maybe, if you're aware of your root issues, but you're going to have to work at it. You must aspire to create a relationship that contradicts the negative belief. The problem is that most folks don't know it's happening. They don't get that they're stuck in a negative pattern. In order to repair the damage from the past, one is required to be in the present.

So, how old do I think Miranda was during that conversation? Ten, eight, five years old? I don't know, I just know she wasn't here and now. Where did her brain perceive she was? In school, being shot down by her teacher? At home, being pushed away by dear old dad?

Miranda? Miranda! Where are you? Grab my hand and I'll pull you back! Don't get sucked in by the darkness of the past, Miranda! Fight! Fight to stay here! Fight!

"Fight! Fight!" Oh, crap. That was my outside voice, wasn't it?

Miranda shot me an angry, tear-filled look. Oh God. I would try to explain to her that I'm actually on her side, but I know she wouldn't see or hear me. Not right now.

She grabbed her hand-made Hill Tribe bag and left in a hurry.

"Sorry, kiddo," I whispered. But she was already gone.

Mordant began laughing underneath his breath – that know-it-all chuckle that said "Smooth move, Ex-Lax."

"Oh! Mister sensitivity! How can you laugh at this poor girl in her hour of need?"

"I'm not laughing at her. I'm laughing at you. What was that? I think you could have been just a touch more insulting if you had ordered popcorn and blatantly enjoyed the show." And he laughed that laugh again. I know his heart went out to the both of them and this was his way of saying "Hey sister, you were just out of line." It's his romantic side – gets the better of him every time. He likes chick flicks, too.

"Very funny. I lost my mind for a minute and now this poor girl thinks we made fun of her," I said.

"We? By we, you mean you?"

"No. By we, I mean us. Ever heard of guilt by association?" I just stared at him. Finally, he gave in. "Great. What now, Kemosabe?" he said.

"We head to the nearest wat."

"What? Oh, wat. Right. Why? I thought we were going to book stores this morning," he said.

"Let's go do some practice and maybe I can shake this weird feeling and the hangover from last night. Then we can shop for a bit."

"Embarrassing yourself in public makes you want to meditate? And you still call it "Practice." You're such a freak."

"Right now, this little girl thinks her boyfriend has abandoned her and two complete strangers belittled her. That's awful, Mordant. I can't believe you don't feel badly about what happened."

"I'd rather go book hunting," he retorted.

Again, I stared.

"Fine," he said. "Practice, then book hunting."

Again, I just stared at him. But this time I was thinking. I knew something was going to happen, but I wasn't exactly sure what, how, or when.

## CONTROL FREAKS

**The way of the sage is to do his duty, not to strive with anyone.**

-Laozi

**He who conquers men has force. He who conquers himself has insight.**

-Laozi

## CONTROL³ (kuhn-trohl)

➤ to govern
➤ to restrain
➤ to regulate

---

3     The New Lexicon Webster's Dictionary of the English Language 1988 Lexion Publications Inc. page 212

## FREAK[4] (freek) - Slang.

➤ A person or animal malformed in a way which makes him or it an object of curiosity.

## RUN! Head for the hills! Look busy!

There is a point of view that says humans spend a lot of time either dominating or avoiding the domination of other human beings. We bet a Control Freak wrote that. If you want to be relieved of the attention-junkie aspect of your personality, just hang out with a Control Freak for a while. It's amazing how being ignored can become so appealing.

Control Freaks often go unrecognized by even the most intelligent people. They have spent a ridiculous amount of time learning how to persuade others to subscribe to their point of view. They want this not because what they say makes sense, but rather, for the sheer control of it. Control Freaks tend to be extreme. All or nothing. In Taoism we say, "not too much, not too little." So when an Overbearing Control Freak decides to run your life, it's all or nothing. Oh, sure, it may start slow, but eventually they will determine what's good, bad, right, and wrong for you. You may protest, but resistance is futile.

Not only will they feel qualified to make decisions for you, they will offer concrete evidence to support their position. It is important to remember that an Overbearing Control Freak thrives on debate. If you allow yourself to engage in one, may the Force be with you. Some Control Freaks have come frighteningly close to mastering verbal Tai Chi. They will try to use your own energy to throw you off-balance, making you vulnerable to doubting your position. A strong Control Freak could convince you that snakes really do have lips and that as soon as you're done painting those snake lips, you should grab a pillowcase, go out to the woods, and wait for that Snipe.

This sounds a lot like a Persecutor, but there are important differences. For example, a Control Freak doesn't always use insults or negativity to claim their spot as king of the hill. There is a difference between a debate and an insult. Let's press on.

---

4    The New Lexicon Webster's Dictionary of the English Language 1988 Lexion Publications Inc. page 376

Command over lifestyle and environment can come into play with this Personality. Ever have your sweetie come in while you were watching your favorite television program, grab the remote (this is the overbearing aspect), and switch to something else?

They may intelligently explain that the news is more important than *I Love Lucy* and that it would better for you to change channels now. Hard to argue, and now you're watching CNN. A Control Freak gets their energy from controlling their environment.

Why is it so important for a Control Freak to have dominion over everything and everybody? It's about feeling safe and secure. Control Freaks are closet fraidy cats. They just have an aggressive way of showing it. The desire to control others is frequently a sign of poor internal structure and low self-image. If the environment feels out of control, a Control Freak tries to tame it. The result of which is about as effective as putting the wind in a jar.

Another frightening fact is that there are degrees to Control Freakism. There is the Overbearing Control Freak – the societal cliché on whom we've already spent enough time. There is also the more ninja-like, Passive-Aggressive Control Freak, and then there are a plethora of "Freaks" in between.

Since we've already discussed the Overbearing Control Freak, we would like to take a moment and discuss the qualities of the Passive-Aggressive Control Freak. Some people can actually control a situation by playing the role of "the victim" or "the martyr." There is a very clear, defining line between our Passive-Aggressive Control Freaks and true Victims. Pay attention!

**A Victim honestly believes they have no control over any given situation. A Passive-Aggressive Control Freak feigns victimization in an attempt to control or manipulate the people around them. This difference is huge!!**

In actuality, these insidious Control Freaks are quite calculated and are banking on your kind heart and your sympathetic disposition so they may manipulate your decision-making process. These Control Freaks literally set up situations where they appear victimized. Very sneaky, but very effective. When someone comes to save them, the Control Freak has won the game by gaining attention, and thus controlling their environment. We know this sounds insane, but if you think about it, you probably know someone who does this.

Again, there are a plethora of Freaks in between the Overbearing Control Freak and the insidious, hard to spot, Passive-Aggressive Control Freak. Whether it is through passive distraction or blatant disapproval, Control Freaks eventually drain Chi.

## Why Me?

Now, what about the recipients of such irritating behavior? Why would anybody want to date a manipulative monster? We have an answer for that question. Read on if you dare. In our experience, there are a number of reasons why a person would date a Control Freak:

1. *To avoid making decisions.*

As we have already discussed, some people simply don't want the responsibility of making choices. In certain situations this works and there's nothing wrong with it. There are Personality Types who would prefer to let someone else make the important decisions. These people are very comfortable allowing someone else to make choices they would rather not deal with (such as issues regarding financial security, lifestyle, etc.). In exchange for this, they provide support for their partner and are happy to do whatever it takes to pick up the slack while their partner is "controlling" everything.

On the downside, this can turn ugly if the person who has chosen to be controlled has collaborated with someone who manifests negative results. If the person in charge (the Control Freak) does not manifest a positive lifestyle, those who choose not to make decisions for themselves get stuck in the mire of their partner's failure. Well, think about it; excessive relinquishment of control is just as perilous as excessive control.

2. *To recreate a cherished relationship.*

It is quite common for people raised with older siblings to be attracted to a Control Freak in a subconscious attempt to recreate the comforts of home. Sounds silly, but it happens. These older siblings were the great protectors when things got rough.

We know you don't really want to date your brother or sister, so a great remedy for this is to volunteer as a Big Brother or Big Sister (or the equivalent in your country) and consciously switch roles for a while. You can learn more about becoming a Big Brother or Sister at www.bbbsa.org.

3. *Because you are a Control Freak, too.*

On occasion, Control Freaks successfully date each other. They actually "get off" on each other's ridiculous manipulations. Think about it! Since Control Freaks love the thrill of debate, they can argue with each other all night long and the fun never ends. Frequently these couples swap roles between the Overbearing and the Passive-Aggressive in an attempt to manipulate or change each other's mind. If you're not a Control Freak, you will not find this entertaining. But, if you are, this is the ultimate kink!

4. *A change of pace*

Sometimes Victims date Overbearing Control Freaks instead of Persecutors for a menu change – all the victimization, half the abuse. Overbearing Control Freaks are Persecutor Light. Passive-Aggressive Control Freaks and Victims sort of cancel each other out, though.

## But seriously folks . . .

The only way to deal with a Control Freak is to acknowledge their opinion and stand behind what you believe to be right for you. Most of us have moments of being a dreaded Control Freak. Some of our favorite people have very strong personalities and easily slide into the stubborn role of the Control Freak. Remember, there are degrees of Control Freakism; one person's Control Freak is another's "stubborn." If there was any Personality Type from our list that you should consider dating and accepting the way that they are, it is the Control Freak – only because if you cut all of them out of your life, you probably won't have many people left to date.

# WHY REAL WOMEN DRINK STRAIGHT TEQUILA
## -Part 2-

Mordant and I left The Sawatdee Cup surrounded by the crackling, electric air of Chiang Mai in the morning. We walked in self-absorbed silence, aware of each other, but not particularly engaged. Within minutes, we found one of the enormous gilded city wats, removed our shoes in continued silence, and made our way up the steps. For those who do not know, a wat is a Temple. Most of Thailand is Buddhist, so the temples are of this ilk.

At the top of the stairs were two huge carved doorways. The doors were open, and inside we could already see the 20 foot tall golden Buddha surrounded by at least a dozen kneeling, faithful believers. There are no benches or chairs in a Thai temple. A Buddhist may come to pray at the foot of the Buddha any time. They simply take off their shoes and kneel on the carpeted area provided. They may stay as long as they need to.

I never thought much of it until I traveled Asia with my Catholic friend. She was always polite, but left each temple as soon as she examined the artwork. I, on the other hand, always take a moment to meditate and pray. Any opportunity to worship is an opportunity well taken by this Tao gal. When asked, my pal simply said, "I appreciate other belief systems, but I draw the line at kneeling." Interesting.

Anyhow, on occasion, there is the equivalent of a church "service," and one may choose to participate. This usually involves the head monk speaking while others listen and pray. I have heard singing; I can only assume these are devotional tunes as beautiful monks always sing them in Thai.

Once inside, Mordant and I went in two different directions and chose spots to kneel apart from each other. For me, the moment I kneel down and close my eyes, I am alone with my maker. So, I prayed. I asked the Universe to explain to me why these total strangers riveted me. I asked the Universe to show me what I was supposed to learn by this strange attraction. And then it occurred to me to ask what happened to me in the moments before I shouted the word "Fight" at that girl.

I saw a picture of The Sawatdee Cup in my mind. I saw the young couple seated at their table. I could not see their faces, but knew it was them. Immediately, I had the overwhelming sense that something was trying to reach Miranda through me. More pictures came . . .

I saw Miranda as a sweet and lively little girl. She was outside, seated at a picnic table. On the table there was a watercolor paint set, and Miranda was painting a picture. It was a tree with flowers all around it. She must have been about six years old.

She jumped up and brought the wet painting over to an adult male. She stood right in front of him and waited for his attention. But, he was engaged in conversation with a woman and did not show the slightest interest in the little girl. In an attempt to show the man the painting, little Miranda lifted the paper over her head with both hands. Suddenly, her foot slipped, she fell forward, and she and the wet painting smashed into the man full force. She recovered quickly, but had torn the paper and smeared paint all over this man's cream-colored shirt. The man abruptly broke his conversation with the woman and focused on Miranda. It took a minute for him to realize that he was covered in paint. He reacted harshly and scolded the girl while wiping his shirt with his hand.

Miranda tried to show her father the torn painting, but it was ruined. She was crushed. So was I. The man then looked directly at me. A single tear fell from his eyes.

"Hey. I'm going outside." A whispering voice in my left ear startled me out of my trance. It was Mordant. I don't know how, but 20 minutes had gone by.

When I left the wat, I felt faint. I know I saw more during that meditation than I recalled, and like a dream, things were already beginning to fade. What did stick with me was that terrible experience with Miranda's father. Poor kid.

I found my sandals and scanned the courtyard. I saw Mordant sitting on a bench facing the street. He was admiring a beautiful Thai woman, so I stayed clear until she had passed. Well, you never know. She could have turned around and stared right back at him. They could have fallen into an ecstatic state of blissful love. She could have taken one look at him and decided she could not take one more step away from this riveting man.

It didn't happen this time, so I walked over to him and sat down on the bench. "Well, you wanna go first?" I said.

"Sure."

"Well?"

"I saw Marcus with another woman," he said.

"Really? I saw Miranda as a little girl. She was with her Dad, and it wasn't good. How old was Marcus? Where was he?"

"I'd peg Marcus in his late twenties, and he was handing flowers to a young Thai woman right there about two minutes ago." Mordant pointed to the gate that led to the compound we were currently sitting in. "They're inside that restaurant having lunch right now." He pointed to a quaint little restaurant across the road.

You could have knocked me over with a feather.

"Ballsy strolling about town with another woman when Miranda could walk around the corner at any time. I hate to say it, but when you're right, you're right. He was holding something back from his girlfriend," I said. "And to think my gut reaction to this guy was to trust him. My radar must be broken today."

For a long while, Mordant and I just sat in silence trying to soak it all in. It was starting to feel like one of those divinely led synchronistic adventures. Although I could not figure out why I had been so engaged in this drama, I could feel the pull of the Universe.

A few minutes later, Marcus and a Thai girl walked out of the restaurant. She had a white paper bag in one hand and a small bouquet of flowers in the other. Marcus took the bag. I assumed it was lunch.

Lunch. *Lunch!* Oh, crap!

"Mordant, what time is it?" I cried.

"About ten to noon. Why?"

"I have a lunch date with Marissa at noon! Oh my God! I have to catch a tuk-tuk and get over to the restaurant. Shit!"

And with that, I took off. Mordant shouted, "Hey, you never told me what you saw?" and then, "Meet me at The Roof Top at 5pm and we'll grab some grub and finish this conversation."

I was in too big a hurry to stop and answer. I ran to the street and started frantically waving down a tuk-tuk. As always, one pulled over in about a minute. I got inside and started telling the driver where I wanted to go. Just before the driver ok off, I looked to my right and almost fainted.

Mordant's face was about six inches from mine. He smiled and said, "You forgot this." And he handed me my purse. Then he said, "Why do I feel like I'm stuck in the middle of something *you* started?"

"Are you mad?" I asked feeling suddenly sheepish.

"Strangely, no."

"Glad to hear it. Be a dear and follow those two if you can. If they fall on the ground and wildly hump in a bush, I want to hear all about it."

"Yeah, right. Then I'll go find his girlfriend and we'll have a big chat," he said sarcastically and started laughing. "Tell Marissa I said hello. And give that crazy husband of hers a big hug. Tell him I want Cuttle Fish in Black Ink Sauce when we come for dinner this week." Mordant patted my purse. "See you at 5 o'clock."

Mordant was still laughing as the tuk-tuk took off. After it left, he started to walk in the direction of Marcus and the young Thai girl.

# THE FANTASY ADDICT

**It is not wise to shine like jade and resound like stone chimes.**

**-Laozi**

**Sincere words are not sweet. Sweet words are not sincere.**

**-Laozi**

## FANTASY [5](fan-tuh-see) n
➢ playful imagination, fancy
➢ a grotesque mental image

## ADDICT[6] (ad-ikt)
➢ to habituate
➢ to have given oneself up to and be or become unduly dependent on
➢ a person addicted to something harmful, usually a drug

Yee haw!  Chivalry is not dead.  Not by a long shot.  If you want proof, date a Fantasy Addict.  They will wine you, dine you, write songs and poetry about you, and put you on a pedestal so high you are sure to get a nosebleed.  And bleed you will unless you're prepared, of course.

Your basic Fantasy Addict is probably the easiest to figure out. Fantasy Addicts are most recognizable by their ability to become whatever their fantasy target wants them to be.  These people are Morphs.  Really!  If you're into strong personality types, that's what they are.  If you prefer a cool intellectual, that's what they are.  Class clown, done.  And if you're looking for your dream lover, look no further.  Your Fantasy Addict will hold you in their arms and insist you look them in the eyes while they tell you how no one has ever made them feel this way before.

They will tell you that only now are they ready to reveal what is in their heart.  Their spirit soars at the thought of sharing their deepest, darkest secrets with you and only you.  For you are the person they've dreamed of all their life.  Yes, indeed they have seen

---

5    The New Lexicon Webster's Dictionary of the English Language 1988 Lexion Publications Inc. page 340

6    The New Lexicon Webster's Dictionary of the English Language 1988 Lexion Publications Inc. page 9

you in their dreams since childhood. From the moment they set eyes on you, they knew you were the one. Their soul mate. All this, on the first date.

Now remember, we're all adults here. As long as nobody is getting hurt and we all know what's going on, then go all out. As long as you never lose sight that these people live in la-la land and that this is a temporary situation, party on.

However, if you find that you can no longer pretend to believe the fairy tales coming from your Fantasy Addict's mouth, the only way to deter their advances is to get real on 'em. Fantasy Addicts die like vampires in the sun when faced with reality. What holy water is to a creature of the night, truth is to a Fantasy Addict. That being said, occasionally it is nice to go out with somebody who blows your attributes completely out of proportion; someone who makes you feel like Cinderella at the ball. But understand now that you have the ability be Cinderella at any time. You choose to feel as though this person made you feel like a rock star. The truth is, if you are looking for someone to make you feel better about yourself, you need only look in the mirror.

## Why Me?

Fantasy Addicts are perfect for you if you are looking for a fun way to avoid intimacy. On some level, each of us has a sense of whom we are dealing with. Those who willingly date Fantasy Addicts are making the choice to keep things at the shallow end of the pool. They stand firm in a relationship whose only boundary is depth. If this is you, then you are going to have some powerful experiences, but they will be with an intimate stranger. We know people who have fabulous sex with strangers, but make no mistake; this is fantasyland, not true intimacy.

Also, these are great transition lovers. If you've just finished a relationship and are feeling a little low, grab a Fantasy Addict for a while and just relax. As long as you're not truly available, they can be an amazing respite from intimacy.

And if you just figured out your lover is full of shit, you can't blame the Fantasy Addict for throwing the party when you signed them on to have it in the first place. There's no mystery, no duping, and any lies that you might have fallen for are only painted scenery on the villa you've been willingly renting by dating them in the first place. There are no victims here either, and there certainly should be no surprises.

If you can't blame the Fantasy Addict for a relationship that is all fluff and no substance then who's responsible? That's right. It's you...again.

## But seriously folks . . .

You want to know why we can't date Fantasy Addicts for a prolonged period? It's because it takes too much Chi. It takes Chi to maintain that willing suspension of disbelief. It takes Chi to pretend that we're okay with wading hip-deep in bullshit – even if it's our own. When dating a Fantasy Addict, you will know their name and various other necessary details (which they usually say they have shared with no one else), but you will never truly know their heart, mind, or soul. You will only find these elusive gems in less turbulent, far deeper waters.

We all want a little romance in our lives, but there comes a time when the burping, and scratching, and (heaven forbid) farting, and bill paying become a necessary evil in every evolving relationship. If you become involved with a Fantasy Addict, you are in for a prolonged honeymoon, true. But, you are also missing the opportunity for a relationship that breaks beyond the surface to something deeper. That spot of heaven where the relationship is more teamwork than tryst. It is here you discover that though the person you are with may not be your fantasy, they certainly are a dream come true.

There is a time and place for everything, so if you need to take a vacation, feel free to take a Fantasy Addict with you. They will make your holiday a memorable one. But remember, when the vacation is over, leave your dashing Fantasy Addict in the fairy tale book where they belong.

≈ ≈ ≈

## WHY REAL WOMEN DRINK STRAIGHT TEQUILA
### -Part 3-

I was about five minutes late for lunch with Marissa. That's pretty good for me. I'm late for everything except work. She didn't notice. She was just finishing logging the last of the lunch receipts when I walked in.

"Hey girlfriend, works over. Let's eat!"

Marissa looked up and smiled. "Just a minute. Do you mind if we all go? Angelo got a little jealous. He says you only come to town once a year and he wants to see you, too."

How could I say no?

Angelo and Marissa own the best Italian restaurant in Chiang Mai. If you're ever there, go to Piccola Roma and tell them Sarina sent you. I've been to Italy and I'm telling you this is the real deal.

In no time at all we were packed into Angelo's car and headed for a five star hotel. We went straight to the restaurant upstairs and were seated at a large round table. Angelo did most of the ordering, though Marissa and I chose a few items as well. As we waited for our meal, Angelo and Marissa began discussing details of the dinner menu that evening. My mind drifted.

I remembered another piece of my meditation from earlier that day. I saw myself this time. No, I felt myself. It was more of a sensation than a picture. I was the hub of a wheel. There were spokes emanating from me in all directions. For a brief moment, I understood how we're all connected. And then, in a jolt of color, I saw my mother. She must have been about 25 years old. Her marriage to my father had ended and she was just barely making ends meet. She was telling me that she could no longer afford to have me live with her, and that Grandma and Grandpa would be taking care of me for a while. I was four years old.

Pictures of life with the grandparents flashed vividly through my brain. I remembered the constant influx of foster children, some of which had fatal diseases. I was never alone. My room had two beds: a spare and mine. The spare bed occupants were ever revolving.

Grandma was the world's worst cook; I remembered that, too. If you've ever eaten your cereal with water instead of milk, you know what it was like for me. When I lived with Mom I ate really yummy stuff. We were poor so we ate mostly vegetarian, but it was always tasty and frequently adventurous. Mom cooked like the Spanish/ Turk that she is. I swear that woman could make a feast with a glass of water and a toothpick. Grandma, on the other hand, should never have been allowed in the kitchen. The pictures faded and I was back in the restaurant with Marissa and Angelo. They didn't seem to notice I had left. I pondered the connection between the little girl with the painting and me.

"I don't get it." Damn it, it's my frickin' outside voice again.

"What?" said Angelo.

I just stared at him. Luckily, I was saved by a huge cart filled with small covered dishes as the beautiful waitress prepared to deliver our feast. It was really something. There must have been a dozen items. Small bowls of soup were placed in front of us. The rest of the dishes were placed on a large Lazy Susan in the middle of the table. There was chicken, seafood, steamed vegetables, Thai noodles, and a variety of things that I could not identify, but which tasted divine with rice. So we ate and we talked for hours.

Lunch concluded with tea, sweet sticky rice with mango, and a variety of weird jelly looking bite sized sweets. I thought I was going to explode when I excused myself from the table to go to the ladies room.

Marissa had packed a doggie bag for me and handed it to me, telling me to go directly downstairs and they would meet me there. So, off I went, snacks in tow to the hotel lavatory.

The ladies room door was directly across from the men's room. They were facing each other in fact. So when I bolted out of the door and smacked into a man who was exiting the men's room, we were face to face. But only for a minute. We hit so hard that the contents of my doggie bag exploded. The force of the crash knocked me back. Luckily, the bathroom door had quickly shut behind me, and I hit the door instead of the floor. You'll never guess whom I bumped into. Yep. Marcus, in the flesh.

"Oh my god. I'm so sorry," he said. It suddenly dawned on me that he had an American accent. I don't think that registered before. "Are you ok?"

"Uh, yeah." I looked down at my shirt. This action caused a barely noticeable twinge of pain along the back of my head and neck. I unconsciously put my hand to my neck and winced. The bag had ripped and some of it's now loose contents were splashed across my shirt. "Except that part where I have food all over me." I said, "I think I banged my head against the door, too." Yes, on closer inspection, that was defiantly pain coming from the back of my head.

"Let me take a look at your head and neck," he said.

Who the heck does this guy think he is, Marcus Welby, MD?

"Just what are your qualifications, sir?" The moment I said it I started laughing.

## INTEGRITY[8] (in-teg-ri-tee)

➤ to bring together or incorporate into a whole
➤ to make up, combine, or complete to produce a whole or a larger unit)

## SYNDROME[9] (sin-drohm)

➤ a group of symptoms that together are characteristic of a specific condition, disease, or the like
➤ the pattern or symptoms that characterize or indicate a particular social condition

Other than Abusers, these scoundrels are by far the worst type of offenders. A Low Integrity Syndrome Person (L.I.S. from here on) is a person who lies. Whether it be a lie invented to manipulate feelings, hide something, or a lie designed to manipulate an outcome, our position is simple: Good relationships are based on trust, and where there are lies, trust cannot grow. Period.

Like the Control Freak, the L.I.S. may try to persuade you to perform all kinds of uncomfortable acts. This ensures our L.I.S. person that you have indeed been suckered and they can move forward with their dastardly plot.

Like the Fantasy Addict, the L.I.S. will sweep you off your perfect little feet. The thing that separates this Personality Type from the others is that while they're working their magic on you, they're spewing the same crap to any number of other unsuspecting conquests (A conquest is not necessarily a lover, but infidelity tends to be part of the package).

Our favorite line comes from a L.I.S. male we know. At the time he was dating a friend of ours, and we relayed to him that it really bugged us that he was so obviously attracted to women other than our friend. Now get this: his ridiculous response was, and we quote, "Guys, I just take all that sexual energy and save it for my girl." Three months later he had an affair.

Why do the L.I.S. do the voodoo they do? Low Integrity Syndrome usually stems from low self-esteem. They don't want anyone to see what they're really all about. The L.I.S. has a need to create an imaginary world they think you'll like better than the reality they actually live in.

---

8    The New Lexicon Webster's Dictionary of the English Language 1988 Lexion Publications Inc. page 692

9    The New Lexicon Webster's Dictionary of the English Language 1988 Lexion Publications Inc. page 1333

There are many levels, ways, and reasons the L.I.S. plays their game. Some will subtly flirt with your friends while others go all out and just plain cheat. Keep your eyes open. Watch for the telltale signs. If you don't like the way your sweetie cozies up to strangers, pay close attention to your body's reaction. If you want to puke, do it, on them. If they drop out of sight for periods of time, don't answer calls, come home late on a regular basis, tell you not to drop by without calling, change their story constantly, tell you they will call and then don't, stand you up for no apparent reason and constantly offer outrageous alibis . . . *Wake up! You've got yourself one bonafied L.I.S. asshole.*

Again, not all L.I.S. people are guilty of infidelity. Some of these horrible creatures are flat out con-men/women. This is how they survive. Many want money, housing, or some other tangible item. We have also seen people make up stories about their life to appear like something they are not.

## Why-oh-why would we...

Date such an unsavory, disloyal, disrespecting lout? It usually has a lot to do with our need to be right.

Now, follow the logic for a minute. If your "story" is that people you love betray your trust, you need an L.I.S. person to make you right. Dating a loser proves your point. You failed, but you didn't deserve it. So, if you have dated more than one person with L.I.S., chances are they aren't the only one with a problem.

For those who honestly got conned, we are terribly sorry. Every once in a while, we run into a psychopathic liar, a person who lies so often they actually begin to believe their own lies. If they believe what they're saying, you'll probably believe them, too.

## But seriously folks . . .

Regardless, don't allow yourself to forget the way your gut reacted to lies. Armed with experience, you never have to go through that again. Whereas reality is the stake in the heart for a Fantasy Addict, the only defense against the Low Integrity Syndrome individual is to turn around and walk away. If you can't walk away, go talk to a professional. You have a problem. If you knew how to fix it on your own, you would have by now. Get help and move on. You deserve better.

# WHY REAL WOMEN DRINK STRAIGHT TEQUILA
## -Part 4-

Mordant here. After Sarina left the temple, I had a few hours to kill, so I walked back toward The Sawatdee Cup and thought I'd look for an English-to-Thai translation book. I prayed I wouldn't actually see Marcus and his Thai tart. I wanted to shake off the weird feeling the morning goings on had left me with. I love books. They love me. We never fight. We never even disagree. Books are my friends. And besides, if I'm nestled in a little bookstore, Sarina and her weird synchronicity Chi can't get me, right?

Who am I kidding? I do Chi Kung, too. Heck, I'm the guy who images Rock Star Parking before he goes shopping and gets it. Oh, yeah. I'm one connected dude.

I asked myself why I'm so connected to this crazy drama. Truth is, I asked the Universe to show me a sign, and then Marcus showed up again. But, does that really mean anything? It's a small town. Maybe it was a coincidence, but I had this creepy feeling the fun had just begun.

Thank goodness I never did run into those two, and when I found a great little bookshop, I stepped inside. It had a box where traveling folks could deposit a book they had finished and trade in for one someone else left. What a great idea! Unfortunately, people from all over the world come here; over half the books were not in English. From the looks of things, German people must really like Chiang Mai.

I was standing at the window, book in hand. It was *He's Just Not That In To You* by Greg Behrendt and Liz Tuccillo, and guess what? I had a feeling someone was looking at me. I jerked my head up and there she was, looking at her reflection in the window. She couldn't see me and I had time to duck.

While crouching, I took a moment and tried to absorb the ramifications of my situation. Miranda, a girl who probably hates me (guilt by association just now having profound meaning in my life), was about two feet away from me.

Okay, Mordant, take stock. First, I didn't ask for this adventure – or did I? Second, I have absolutely no connection with this woman – or do I? Third, even if I go out there and talk to her, I wouldn't know what to say – or would I?

"Excuse me, sir. Are you alright?" A young Thai man was bending over and looking at me with concern.

"Uh, fine," I said, standing to hand him the book. "I'll take this, please."

I finished my purchase and assumed I would walk outdoors to a Miranda-less street. I was wrong. She was sitting outside a little bar sipping something and staring into space. I tried to walk by very quietly so as not to disturb her.

"Your girlfriend is pretty rude," she said as I tried to sneak by.

"She's not my girlfriend. Everyone thinks she is, but she's not. After Europe, I just couldn't... Oh. Sorry. Hey, she didn't mean anything by it, Miranda."

"You know my name?"

"You two were pretty loud. It was hard *not* to know your name." And your boyfriend's name, and your itinerary, and your personal problems, and your coffee preference... "Sorry she upset you. She looked for you after you left so she could apologize."

"That's okay," Miranda said. "This is the worst day of my life. There isn't really anything else that could happen to screw it up." And with that, an intelligent gust of wind blew her purse and its contents right off the table.

Without thinking, I bent down, scooped up her belongings, and gave them back before she had a chance to move. We just looked at each other for a minute, and then started laughing.

"Hey, you know, I'm not really that crazy. This whole vacation has been so weird. You want a tea or something?"

"Uh, am I one of those guys you're 'looking' at, doll?" I raised my eyebrows and tried to look mature and wise. I have strong feelings about dishonesty. Cheating is bad, even if it's between a hottie and me. I suppose Sarina never mentioned that Miranda is definitely a hottie.

"No! I was just saying that. I would never cheat on anybody." The look on her face told me this was the truth. I sat down.

"Then, why did you say that?"

"I don't know! Everything was fine when we got here. We traveled down south for a little bit and then made our way up here so Marcus could go to Thai Massage School. When he found out how much it cost, he had to drop the idea. He was so disappointed. Right after that, he started going for walks without me. Within a few days he got a job teaching English; he said it was so we could have a little extra spending dough and stay longer. He is usually very cryptic about where and who he's teaching. I stopped believing him two weeks ago. When I ask him about it, he tells me there's nothing to tell. He says I should go get a massage, walk around, and hang by the pool. You know, Chiang Mai stuff. But I wanted to do these things with him. He hates me now!" And with that, Miranda started to cry; again.

I shouted louder than normal, "Waiter! Can we get two Thai ice teas and a menu please?" This place was cool. There were only two wait staff watching us. "Heeeeey. No more tears. It'll be alright," I said kindly.

"Thank you, but you don't need to coddle me. I'm hurting, not helpless."

"Okay then. Miranda, before I decide that you are definitely hanging with the wrong guy, tell me one thing." I leaned in close and looked her straight in the eyes. "Is there any validity to Marcus's compliant that you are too needy?"

"He never said that!" she darned near shouted.

"No, but that's what he meant. Look, it sounds like you just got involved with a dud, but I want to be sure. So tell me, is there any truth to the accusation that you have changed since you got here and have become a little clingy?"

Heavy sigh from Miranda.

"Maybe."

"Maybe?"

"Well, I have to admit that when he started pushing me away, I started wanting him more. But I think that's normal. We all want what we can't have, right? I mean, at home – we live together in Los Angeles – he's so attentive. As a matter of fact, he's the one who's usually chasing me now that I think of it."

"And how do you react to him while he's available to you? Do you love and need him as much as you do today?"

Miranda started playing with her fingers again. The waiter brought two ice teas and menus. Miranda already knew what she wanted.

"One national dish please." The waiter was silent. Miranda suddenly broke in to a hearty laugh. "I just love doing that. Pad Thai, please, with chicken."

I handed the unopened menus back and said, "That sounds great. Make it two."

Miranda and I sat for a few minutes and watched the tourists as they wandered about looking at "stuff." Thailand is famous for it's shopping, by the way. You have to experience it to really get it. I know people who come here just to buy "stuff" and bring it back to America to sell. Heck, I've even done it. Wasn't that long ago I was selling sarongs I bought here to people back home.

I looked back at Miranda who was obviously deep in thought.

"Penny for your thoughts," I said, breaking the silence.

"I was just thinking about all the times when I was younger," she said, "and all those boys who chased me. I was hard on them. Maybe this is my payback. Maybe it's my turn to feel the pain of rejection." And once again, Miranda started to cry. This time, I let her.

I didn't really know what to say. So I excused myself and went to the men's room to wash my hands and think. I knew something she didn't. I knew he was messing around. Or did I? I saw Marcus walk into a building with a Thai girl. I saw him walk out a few minutes later with the same girl. Were they holding hands? Damn! I don't remember. Am I leading this sweet girl down the wrong path? I want to help, but I'm not sure where to go from here.

I left the men's room more confused than ever.

When I returned, lunch had arrived. I noticed Miranda had not only stopped crying, but also she had the good manners to wait for me before she started eating.

"Please, go right ahead," I said as I sat down. "Ok, one more question before I pass judgment." Which is funny, because I make it a point not to do that in my personal life. "What do you really think he's up to? Do you think he's messing around?" I asked.

Miranda stopped eating and looked at me.

"Absolutely not. You don't know my Marcus. He's not perfect, but he's not like that. I have been weird with him since we got here, and that's what's turning him off." She sat back as though she had just heard this concept for the first time. It just sank in. "You know, when he first started teaching, he invited me to come help him tutor someone, and I refused to go because I was angry." Her eyes began turning red. The truth was coming out. Marcus did try to share his experience with her. She was just such a drag, he never offered again. "He hasn't invited me to join him since. He probably thinks I'll embarrass him. He doesn't trust me any more and he doesn't want to share his experiences with me either. God, I'm such an ass."

Maybe. But does that give him permission to cheat and lie? Oh, Miranda, things are far more complex than you think. Sarina? Where are you?

66

## THE CO-DEPENDENTS

> If you realize that all things change, there is nothing you will try to hold on to.  If you aren't afraid of dying, there is nothing you can't achieve.
>
> -Laozi

> Trying to control the future is like trying to take the master carpenter's place.  When you handle the master carpenter's tools, chances are you will cut your hand.
>
> -Laozi

**DEPENDENT[10] (di-pen-duhnt)**
➤ depending on someone or something else for aid or support
➤ conditioned or determined by something else

Co-Dependents are kind of neat because they will cover up for your mistakes; that's what they do best. Some will shred you for your behavior in private, but all of them will lie on your behalf in a social situation thus making ill behavior much easier.

Co-Dependants date Addicts, Liars (L.I.S. people), and Abusers almost exclusively. Addicts, Liars, and Abusers have secrets and usually require some damage control in order to maintain the respect of the community.  A hallmark of a Co-Dependant is that they think they are martyrs for putting up with your crap.  They appear to be "Fixers" on the outside, but on further examination, are actually *contributors to the problem*.

## Why, oh why would I date a Co-Dependant person?

---

10   The New Lexicon Webster's Dictionary of the English Language 1988 Lexion Publications Inc. page 356

People date Co-Dependants because they aren't ready to get well and take responsibility for their life. Did you know that many Co-Dependant partners of alcoholics drink with their partner? Some will even buy the booze. Sure, they'll bitch and moan that life is hell with a using alcoholic, but they don't leave. Yup, that's right; Co-Dependents will threaten to leave you if you don't get your shit together, but they never do. Nope. Instead they'll hang around and help you continue growing into your problem.

## But, seriously folks...

Only you can tell if your sweetie is turned on or off by your dysfunctions. Only you know if they feed the demon or encourage you to tame it.

It's healthy to seek the company of someone who accepts us the way we are. The problem with dating a Co-Dependant person is that they need a serious dysfunction to cover up in order to feel normal. If you are dating a Co-Dependant and get well, they will most likely test your resolve in an effort to maintain the type of relationship they are familiar with. So, if you do it just right, you get to transform your negative pattern and your unhealthy relationship all in one swoop. We hope that your Co-Dependant chooses to transform their dysfunction when you transform yours, so the two of you can stay together.

## WHY REAL WOMEN DRINK STRAIGHT TEQUILA
## -Part 5-

Marcus and I made our way through the streets of Chiang Mai on his red scooter. It was so fun I almost forgot how much I loathed him. Almost. We pulled up in front of a building that read "Thai Massage School" and got off the scooter.

"Come on," Marcus said. "These girls will take excellent care of you."

So, I took off my shoes and in I went. Nothing I hadn't seen before. In Chiang Mai, you can get two hours of Thai massage at one of these places for about $10.00 if you know where to go.

There was about a half dozen Thai girls sitting around and another three or four massaging the feet of customers who were reclining in comfy chairs. By the way, never pay more than about

100 baht (about $3.00) for a one-hour foot massage when in Chiang Mai. Any more than that, and they're taking advantage of the fact that you are an ignorant tourist.

"Sawatdee khup, ladies," said Marcus.

"Sawatdee kah," most of them replied in unison. This made them all laugh.

I smiled, but inside I was thinking, "You, sir, are why women become neurotic." I felt instantly sorry I was so hard on Miranda. She was right. Something is going on here and it's not good.

Marcus walked over to an older woman sitting behind the desk.

"Khun Mint, this is, uh . . ." He looked at me.

"Sarina," I said and smiled at her.

"Sarina," Marcus repeated. "She had an unfortunate run-in with a bag of food and a very clumsy man." His smile was so warm, that once again, I forgot how much I hated him. "Would you please look at her neck? And while you're at it, can we get that shirt cleaned up?" Mint looked at me with curiosity. I could see her sizing me up. Probably wondering if I was the girlfriend she was competing with. Wait. This is not the woman I saw coming out of the restaurant with Marcus earlier today. That woman was much younger. Still, I sensed that Khun Mint knew exactly what was going on.

"Why you not wash shirt before you come here?" she inquired.

I hadn't thought about that. Because I wanted to have an excuse to snoop into this guys life? No. That won't work.

"Look at my shirt. If I got it wet, it would be like I'm naked." I smiled at Khun Mint hoping this explanation would resonate with her female sister type side. It did.

"You right," she said. "You get arrested for walking Chiang Mai naked!" Everyone in the room, including the patrons, laughed. I realized everyone in the room was watching us.

"Khun Mint, when Sarina and I ran into each other, she hit her head on a door. Would you please, personally, look at her and be sure she's okay?" Marcus asked.

"No problem. I always like pretty lady to come to my school. Maybe you become my next student?" she replied.

"No thank you, Khun Mint, I am already a massage instructor." I saw Marcus's eyes open wider.

"Ok. Come with me," she said. And with that, she began yelling at the Thai girls in Thai, and three of them jumped up and led me through a curtain in the back of the shop. I glanced back at Marcus, and he said, "Don't worry, Teach. I'll be right here when you get out."

There was a staircase to my right and an old looking sink in front of me. The girls did not speak English well, so they communicated their intention by beginning to undress me. I let them. I felt completely safe. I usually do in Thailand. The big cities have some questionable areas, but, all in all, it's much safer than the States.

After they took my shirt and skirt, the girls dressed me in loose fitting cotton pants and a matching tunic top. This is common for Thai massage. Unlike the American versions, there is no nudity involved in the process. If you take your clothes off for your Thai massage, it is most likely because a prostitute is massaging you and the experience is quite different. I was brought up to a room with eight or ten mats on the ground. Six of the mats had patrons and a masseur on them.

I was led to an open mat and a nice girl motioned to me to lie down, face up. She positioned herself at my head, sat down, slid her cool fingers under my neck, and began massaging. Within minutes, the events of the day began to melt away.

And I remembered more...

I was back at The Sawatdee Cup. This time, I was sitting where Miranda was sitting earlier that day. I recognized the man across from me as the man in my vision; Miranda's father. He was dressed in his cream-colored shirt and it was smeared with paint.

"I'm so sorry, honey. If I had known how my behavior would have affected you, I never would have been so cold," he said. "There's still time, Miranda. You don't have to live the isolated life I led. When your mother passed away, I was so angry..." He stopped. Then, he looked up with a glowing smile and said, "Open your heart, Miranda. Experience life. Let this boy love you. Support him and watch how he rises to the occasion. Fight the urge to repeat your ancestral heritage of pain and victimization. You are here to evolve, my daughter, so undertake to do it joyfully."

Something in the room had shifted. I opened my eyes in time to see Khun Mint positioning herself to work on my neck. The original girl was leaving and I gave her a quiet "Khawp khun kha." That's "Thank you, female form" in Thai. She smiled, said something in Thai, and departed.

Khun Mint was obviously more experienced as she began feeling the vertebrae in my neck. Something was amiss, so she gently pulled on my head, thus stretching my neck, while simultaneously and gently pushing the vertebrae back in to place.

The entire experience was probably 10 minutes. When she finished, she said, "You lay here. I come back for you in little bit. Okay pretty woman?" We smiled at each other and she left me to rest.

I don't know how much time went by, but I awoke to a completely new Thai girl gently shaking me. She had both my skirt and my shirt folded neatly in one hand. She helped me up and led me down the hall to a changing room.

My clothes were perfect. Slightly damp, but in a country where the humidity is frequently at 100%, one grows accustomed. The stains were gone. I had a little perfume in my bag and used a touch to make sure the clothing smelled like me. As I disrobed, I realized I had no pain in my head or neck. As a matter of fact, I felt really great; sort of light.

I put on my flowered skirt and pulled over the cream-colored blouse. There was a mirror in the room, and I did the classic spin to see how it fit. As always, when traveling Asia, I was shrinking. All the soup, veggies and walking just drain the body fat right off. I was satisfied with my fresh appearance and headed out realizing for the first time since I arrived upstairs that I still had Marcus to contend with. I walked downstairs and found Marcus speaking with Mint.

"Mint says you're fine now. Take it easy if you can, though. She had to put your bones back into place." He looked back at Mint. ""Well, I guess this is it." I could swear he was getting a little misty. "Thank you. Thank you for everything, Khun Mint. I hope Lek does better in school, now. Her English has really improved these past few weeks. I had a great time working with her. She's a funny girl!" He smiled boldly and Khun Mint smiled back.

"Now you bring that silly girlfriend back here again, ok?" said Khun Mint.

"Oh! I'm not his girlfriend," I protested.

The room was silent for a minute, and then everyone started laughing again. No one explained a thing as Marcus started guiding me toward the door.

"Oh, we'll be back. Rest assured." And with that, we headed outside to our shoes and the scooter. "Come on," he said. "I'll drop you at The Roof Top. It's almost 4:20."

It was at that point that I noticed a large manila envelope in Marcus's hand. "What's in the envelope, Marcus?" I said, suddenly realizing I had said his name out loud.

"This is my certificate. I just completed a Thai Massage course here. Now I'm a certified Thai Massage practitioner! I can't wait to tell my girlfriend. This whole thing was supposed to be a surprise, but keeping the secret really made her paranoid. I just want to find her now and lay all the cards out on the table."

"I don't understand. How could massage school upset her?" I said.

"Well, when we first arrived I found out the course was twice what I thought it would be, and told my girlfriend that I would have to pass. It was disappointing because we had come so far. Anyways, I came back to the school without her one day to see if I could convince the owner, Khun Mint, to let me take the class and mail her money when I got home. She would not agree to that, but said her niece was failing out of Chiang Mai University and needed an English Tutor. She offered me a flat out trade!"

"Again, why would this upset your girlfriend?" I was fishing for the "because I'm sleeping with my student" answer here. Instead I got:

"Oh, that. Well, my original idea was to tell my girl that I got a job as an English tutor to cover up the fact that I was taking massage class. I wanted to surprise her. It's only a four-week course. I thought I could pull it off." Marcus looked at the envelope and dropped his smile. "It turned ugly so fast," he mumbled.

"I've been living with my girlfriend for two years. In all that time, she has been the more independent of the two of us. But, something happened to her when I started this whole massage thing. It's like she snapped or something. I even invited her to come help me tutor and she refused to have anything to do with it. All she wants to do these days is talk about how I'm abandoning her. It's a *huge* turn off."

"So your answer to the situation is to take Khun Mint's niece, your student, to a fancy hotel and screw her?" I said bluntly.

Marcus's eyebrows furrowed so close together, they damned near became one. Then, he started laughing. "You think I was at the hotel having sex with Lek? You've got to be kidding. Lek is 18 years old and works at the hotel part time. It's just easier working there than going to Doi Saket and trying to find her village and then her house. The hotel is five minutes from the massage school. We have a ritual; we meet at a wat a few minutes away, buy some sticky buns at Lek's favorite shop and walk and talk, in English on the way to the hotel. Then we study for an hour. When we're done, I go to school and she goes to work. We do this three days a week," he said. "At least we did. Today was our last day. I'm done now, see." And with that, Marcus handed me the envelope.

Sure enough, there was a certificate of completion from Thai Massage School inside (That is literally the name of the establishment).

Oh, dear.

"Marcus, would you consider waiting for my friend Mordant at The Roof Top with me? I'll buy."

## THE JEALOUS LOVERS

**High ceremony fusses but finds no response; then it takes to enforce itself with rolled up sleeves.**

**-Laozi**

**JEALOUS**[11] **(je'lus)**
➤ resentful and envious, as of someone's attainments or of a person because of his attainments
➤ fearful of losing another's affection

**LOVER**[12] **(luv-er)**
➤ a person who is in love
➤ a person, who is involved in a non marital affair; paramour

On the one hand, we'd really like to hang these people. On the other hand, this behavior is so common we'd sort of be hanging ourselves. Oh, what the hell.

---

11  The New Lexicon Webster's Dictionary of the English Language 1988 Lexion Publications Inc. page 522.

12  The New Lexicon Webster's Dictionary of the English Language 1988 Lexion Publications Inc. page 794

Jealous Lovers (J.L.) can be a royal pain in the ass. The hard core J.L. are the wackos that look at your brand new outfit and accuse you of secretly using it to pick up other people while you two are on a date. It never crosses their mind that just maybe you bought the outfit to please them. These are also the same people you see slowly driving past your house at two in the morning.

A Jealous Lover has the uncanny ability to show up at the same establishment you're partying at with your friends. Repeatedly. The really flamboyant ones will scream at you in a public place when they finally catch you with someone they've never met. The fact that the individual you were secretly rendezvousing with was your sibling will not save you the embarrassment as you won't be able to get a word in edgewise until it's too late.

The worst part of this Personality Type is that nine times out of ten your Jealous Lover also has the dreaded Low Integrity Syndrome. Yes, it's true. People who don't trust usually can't be trusted. A creative Jealous Lover lulls you into a false sense of security. They lead you to believe that they are obsessively devoted to you when the truth is they are anything but.

There is another kind of monster associated with this Personality Type. Some people have a messed up need to create their lover's jealousy. By this we mean that some people are masters at setting you up to be the jealous one. It's insidious. For example, they'll just sort of mention that their last lover looked just like your best friend. Or maybe they'll jump down your throat when you ask where they were all night.

By averting the real issue over to your nosiness, you will never actually get an answer to your pretty simple question. Once a number of questions go unanswered, you will start to feel nuts, and before you know it everyone becomes suspect: the waitress, the waiter, their "best friend," your best friend – even the gas station attendant.

## Who would date one of these drama kings/queens?

It could be construed as fun for a while to have such an attentive lover but the glitter fades pretty quick. Hate to say it, but most of us have fallen for the adrenaline rush that results from spending time with the Jealous Lover. There is something very ego-satisfying about a person who wants to own us, isn't there? Sort of brings up the primal, caveman side of our nature when someone wants to bang us over the head and drag us to the cave to be ravaged. Oooh!!!

For those who stay in the negative drama of the Jealous Lover, consider your self-worth, dear one. Do you deserve to be spoken to this way? Are you really not to be trusted? Do you trust your partner?

Being treated as if you have done something wrong on a regular basis is a form of emotional abuse. If you are enduring this and the fun has long faded, you are officially in a relationship which lacks intimacy. Yep, once again, the issue is yours and only you can transform the need to be pushed away.

## But seriously folks . . .

If you realize that all things change, there is nothing you will try to hold on to. Unfortunately, there is only one real solution to this dilemma. It is the same solution for dealing with an L.I.S. person. If they don't clean up their act, turn around and walk. You deserve better.

We know how harsh that sounds. You may well be wondering if that's not throwing the babe out with his bath water. We see it like this: you have to have your head on as straight as possible just to get by these days. Jealousy is one of those consuming emotions that cloud the vision so much that we tend to lose our ability to reason cognitively.

When dealing with a Jealous Lover, your entire relationship will eventually be centered on jealousy. You will either be dealing with their ridiculousness or combating your own. Why even get started? But if you really want to test the waters, knock yourself out. Mark our words: after you've knocked yourself out you're going to want to knock them out, too.

# WHY REAL WOMEN DRINK STRAIGHT TEQUILA
## -Part 6-

Miranda and I finished our lunch in almost complete silence. I was uncomfortable because I all but accused her boyfriend of cheating. If Miranda was going to discover the evil truth about her boyfriend, it wasn't going to be from me. I was just debating the best way to exit this situation when Miranda chimed in.

"Hey, have you ever been to the Day Bazaar?"

"You mean the Night Bazaar?" Silly girl.

"No, I mean the Day Bazaar. They just started it. Usually it's just the Sunday Bazaar, but there's something going on this weekend and they're starting it today. It'll run for the next three days." And then she sealed the deal. "It's just across from The Roof Top bar at Tapei Gate."

That pretty much kicked in the psychedelic sensations right there. I looked at my watch. Ten after two. Just enough time to take the leisurely walk to Tapei Gate and shop for a couple of hours before meeting Sarina at The Roof Top. Ooh. If this works out just right, I might even get to see a real cat fight! This time, it didn't even occur to me that Miranda was being inappropriate. But she, who had a propensity for living in the past, put my mind at rest anyway.

"I'm not being weird. Strangers meet and hang out over here all the time. It's just what you do in Thailand if you're a tourist. Marcus and I were even guests at a local's house in Phuket last month for a few days. We slept and ate there. The guy wanted to hang with us constantly, so we ended it sooner than later, though." Forgetting herself, Miranda started laughing. I hoped her laughter would not turn to tears. It didn't.

"Well," I said, "you're certainly feeling better."

"Yeah. I realize that I've been hard on Marcus. I also realize, now, that he is the one I want. Maybe I wasn't appreciative enough when he was chasing me, but I have time to change my creepy, angry behavior while we're here. Of course the needy girl that he's been living with these past weeks turns him off. Honestly, I don't blame him. I don't like that girl too much, either."

This would all be well and good if I hadn't seen that contemptible jerk . . . I mean that lying SOB . . . I mean Marcus, with that woman this morning. I can't remember if they were holding hands, but I will never forget seeing him give that woman flowers. I've been an actor for over twenty years and let me tell you, this guy is good.

"So?" she asked again. "Wanna go shopping?"

"I have to meet Sarina, my rude non-girlfriend, but I have time. So, why not? Okay, Miranda, lead the way."

I paid our bill and secretly wished I had a cell phone to call Sarina and tell her how weird my day was going. She was probably safely tucked away with people she knew having polite conversation while I was living in the Land of the Bizarre Coincidences. She's more accustomed to this level of synchronicity. I used to think she lived in a world exclusive to herself. I see now that we may all request time in this rich and powerful space. Part of me was uncomfortable. Part of me felt the connection between all things. Part of me felt vulnerable. Part of me could not deny that this day was the direct product of my own thoughts and a co-creative effort with something much bigger than myself. I was in awe. When I saw pretty girls, I looked them in the eye and had no fear as I smiled at them. Lo and behold, they smile back. But, more than that, all people looked beautiful to me. All things looked a hint richer. The strange foods from the odd little street carts smelled wonderful and the often toothless cooks looked like something from a travel magazine. It was amazing.

Miranda and I spent the next few hours wandering though crowded streets. There was jewelry, clothing, carvings, and other "stuff" to browse through. I felt a closeness to this girl that went beyond sexuality. I saw Miranda as a young, intelligent woman who would be okay, regardless of how things play out between her and her boyfriend.

As each hour ticked by, I began to see more and more of the real Miranda. She was light and joyful. She marveled at the hand-made trinkets and cooed at little Thai youngsters as they tottered by. This strange and magical place has always worked its mojo on me, too. I felt the shift in my spirit as I walked the streets with my new friend.

"Miranda, I need to tell you something," I said.

"Please don't say anything to ruin my buzz," she said with an innocent smile.

So, she felt it, too. Interesting.

"Sarina is right over there." I pointed to The Roof Top across the street. "She really wanted a chance to explain what happened this morning. All I know is that she wasn't actually shouting at you. She has a propensity these days to get lost in thought, and I think she was just blurting out whatever it was she had on her mind."

"I told you, I don't care," she said, the gloom ever so slightly moving across her pretty, young face.

"No. I know her. She wants a chance to apologize for hurting you. And frankly, dear, I'd like to hear her explain this one, too. I was pretty embarrassed."

Miranda smiled

# PARANOID SCHIZOPHRENICS

**Roses are red, Violets are blue,
I'm schizophrenic, and so am I.**

**-Unknown**

### PARANOIA[13] (par-a-noi-a)
➢ extreme and unreasonable suspicion of other people and their motives
➢ a psychiatric disorder involving systematized elusion, usually of persecution

### SCHIZOPHRENIA (skit-suh-free-nee-uh)
➢ A severe mental disorder in which a person becomes unable to act or reason in a rational way, often with delusions and withdrawal from social relationships

### SCHIZOPHRENIC[14] (skit-suh-fren-ik)
➢ Psychiatry. Also called dementia praecox. a severe mental disorder characterized by some, but not necessarily all, of the following features: emotional blunting, intellectual deterioration, social isolation, disorganized speech and behavior, delusions, and hallucinations.
➢ A state characterized by the coexistence of contradictory or incompatible elements.

Paranoid Schizos (P.S.) are a lot of fun. All the rules that apply to we "normal crazy people" go right out the window. P.S. are named such because they display both paranoia and schizophrenia. Paranoid people have an abnormal tendency to suspect and mistrust. Schizophrenics have, among other things, a propensity

---

13 The New Lexicon Webster's Dictionary of the English Language 1988 Lexion Publications Inc. page 794

14 American Psychological Association (APA): SCHIZOPHRENIA. (n.d.). Dictionary.com Unabridged (v1.1). Retrieved November 14, 2007, from Dictionary. com website: http://dictionary.reference.com/browse/SCHIZOPHRENIA

toward delusions within their personal relationships. Put 'em together and you have one serious, toxic soup. When you hang out with a Paranoid Schizophrenic, eventually you become the subject of their delusional mistrust; and then the fun begins.

Note the difference between a J.L. and a P.S. is that the latter is thoroughly convinced there is something horrible you are hiding, and it doesn't have to be an affair; it could be anything. They are truly paranoid, and it is a trick of the mind which keeps them in misery. You cannot fix a P.S. They usually need professional help in order to have a happy life.

The entertainment value of the whole thing lies in not knowing what triggers a psychotic episode. You never really know what to expect with a P.S. A P.S. will come up with psycho fears that are so left field you have to pinch yourself to make sure whatever it was they just said is what you just heard. It takes absolutely nothing to convince them there is a problem. You're cheating, you're leaving, you're definitely lying. Then, after you cringe, you struggle with the decision of whether or not you want to dignify the fear with a response or hop the next train to Katmandu.

## Why-oh-why... would anyone date a crazy person?

OK, Sarina here. I've got a few answers for that one. Sometimes – not always – the answer to that one is *sex*. Anyone who's ever been to bed with a wildly abandoned person who has focused their outrageous passion on them knows they just do things, uh, different. Not every sexual encounter needs to be wild and crazy, but let's face it, sometimes crazy is sexy as hell. They write movies about that stuff.

Mordant says a reason we date crazy people is because we have a taste for drama. As a child, if you witnessed outrageous behavior from the adults in your life, it's possible that you associate drama with love. If loving a parent proved dangerous, you may be more comfortable with someone a little on the nutsy side. Who's crazy now?

It never ceases to amaze us that some of the most publicly passive people are dating or married to some truly bonkers partners. Their partners are not necessarily bad people. As a matter of fact, they are kind, generous, and truly love their mate. But, behind closed doors, in the face of romantic intimacy, Paranoid Schizophrenics are a lot of work and the work never ends.

Here's the other thing we've noticed. Their partners seem to enjoy the never ending state of engagement in the daily drama. What we're saying is that one of the partners may be fending off imaginary demons, but the other partner is taking it seriously. One is a P.S. while the other is a Co-Dependant. The outcome? A never-ending psycho drama which only interests the two people involved.

## But seriously, folks . . .

If your sweetie is able to laugh at their ridiculous behavior at the end of the day or when it's pointed out to them, there's a really good chance they're worth a second thought. We all have moments of paranoia. Moments.

If you're dealing with someone who can look at their paranoia and recognize it for the pile of rubbish it is, take it as a sign that this person may be going through a growth process, or at the very least, is working on their unfortunate problem. We all have our idiosyncrasies. If you can't talk them down from the "bad place," leave them alone. Try pointing out the delusion later. If you really can't get through, if they really can't laugh at themselves, if they really believe you're out to get them, it's time to examine your attraction to negative drama.

Lastly, if you are dating someone who can't see you for who you really are, they're incapable of intimacy with you. If you find this titillating, it's time to look in the mirror.

# Hornitos™ Bandera Shot

We salute you, dear Mexico. Here's a toast to the green, white and red.

1 shot Hornitos™ Reposado Tequila

1 shot Sangrita

1 shot lime juice

Sip alternately from the three shot glasses. First the lime juice, then the Hornitos™, and finally the Sangrita.

drink 🕱 smart

# WHY REAL WOMEN DRINK STRAIGHT TEQUILA
## -Part 7-

The Roof Top Bar is located across from Tapei Gate in the heart of Chiang Mai. It is three stories up a gross little building, but when you rise up to that third floor, you enter a whole new plane of existence. By about 10 P.M. any night, when the roof is rolled back and stars shine above, interesting visitors from around the world lounge on fluffy pillows on the floor and drink Thai whisky. Tables are about six inches off the ground and are frequently covered with Thai food and beer bottles. And, yeah, you can smoke there.

The Roof Top is a great place to meet people at 10 P.M. At 4:30 P.M., however, it's empty. Open, but empty. The roof hasn't even been rolled back yet. Marcus and I went up, grabbed a couple of pillows, and sat down to chat.

"Do you think it's too early to drink?" he asked.

"Not at all," I said remembering the Thai whiskey hangover that morning. "I'll have a juice. You pick, I'm fine with anything."

"Want some food? I'm starving."

"You get what you want and I'll nibble."

With that, Marcus went to the bar to order. He came back a few minutes later with a platter of shot glasses and a bottle of Hornitos™ Reposado. Two shot glasses were empty, two had lime juice and two had Sangrita. Marcus set the lot down and poured the delicious liquor, filling each of the empty shot glasses to the rim. He explained that you take a sip of lime, then a sip of Hornito's™, and last, a sip of Sangrita (a sweet tomato drink with a spicy kick).

I just stared at him. Of course he chose Hornitos™. No matter how hard I try, I just can't hate this guy.

"The lime and Sangrita count as juice, right?" he laughed as he put three shot glasses in front of me. "This is a celebration."

"To me," he toasted.

"To not judging a book by its cover," I added. And with that we clinked glasses; three times.

"So, now I have a question for you, Sarina."

"Sure."

"How is it I never told you my name, but you seem to know it."

I must have turned five shades of white. Then, the obvious answer came to me.

"I must have heard it from one of the girls at the massage school," I answered confidently.

"Nope. They call me Khun Grasshopper. Everyone calls me that over there, except Khun Mint, who just calls me Grasshopper. So, try again." He was looking at me very intensely, now.

When in doubt, tell the truth. *Whew.* It's a lot easier giving that advice than taking it sometimes. "You don't recognize me, do you?" I said.

"You've looked familiar all day, but I still can't place it. Do we know each other?"

"Not exactly. I was at The Sawatdee Cup this morning. We were right across from each other while you and Miranda were arguing."

The light bulb just went off above this guy's head.

"Oh my God! That was you? Was that Mordant with you?"

"Yep."

He started laughing and then turned serious when he said, "Why didn't you say anything when we first met?"

"Honestly, Marcus, I thought you were cheating on Miranda. I don't know why, but I became drawn into the whole drama this morning at the café. I know it's wrong, but when Mordant saw you give flowers to that girl today, we were convinced you were a jerk."

"You were there? Were you guys spying on me? Did you follow me? Not that it's any of your business, but I was giving flowers to Lek because it was our last day of tutoring and she had done so well." He paused. "So you've been hanging out with me today because you wanted to bust me in a lie. Just what did you think you were going to do when you caught me in the act? Run up to me and say 'Hey! Total stranger! You're a bad person and we know it!'"

He was pissed. He was hurt. I felt like an idiot.

"Look, Marcus, I don't know why Mordant and I were drawn to you and your girlfriend, but we were. My suspicion is that we were brought together to help each other out. For what it's worth, the reason I wanted you to come here was so I could show Mordant how wrong we were about you." I knew my explanation didn't help. Marcus just sat there staring in to space. "Don't you feel it?" I asked quietly.

"What the hell are you talking about?" he snapped.

"Something's going on. What other explanation is there for the constant synchronicities? Marcus, we didn't follow anybody. We went to the wat to meditate. When Mordant stepped outside, you were right there, handing flowers to someone he knew was not your girlfriend. What was he supposed to think?" I took a deep breath and continued, "I think I've had lunch at the Sheraton one other time in over 10 years. Come on, that's just too weird. I had to go with you today, just to see what the hell was going on. There was a reason we were brought together."

Marcus was still bitterly silent.

"Marcus, would you like to know what I saw when I was inside that wat you met Lek at today?"

Marcus looked up sharply. "What do you mean?"

"I told you. I was inside meditating when you and Lek met today. Do you want to know what I saw?"

"Not really. But somehow I don't think I can stop you," he said.

I proceeded to tell Marcus about the visions I had that morning and then throughout the day.

He listened attentively and then said, "Her father passed away three months before we left for Thailand. That's so weird."

He was softening.

"Marcus, I'm convinced he was trying to tell her, through me, that she was just re-experiencing an old pain. When she thought you were abandoning her, she reverted to when she was six years old, being rejected by the man she loved the most: her father. That's why she's been so unrecognizable lately. Although I think it's healthy that you did not find that behavior attractive, I have to believe the woman you fell in love with still exists in that body. I think I was given the information because I understand. I felt the pangs of old rejections, too. I see now that, like it or not, I may have reacted the same way. That's why I found her so distasteful at the café this morning. It was too much like looking in the mirror.

"Anyhow, that's why I kept running into you all day. Her father wants both of you to know he's sorry, Marcus, and he wants his little girl to open her heart; *to you.*"

Marcus sat in stunned silence. I felt completely drained. I did not feel sick, just exhausted. The room was fuzzy and I could not muster another word. Suddenly, Marcus stood up.

"I'm not mad, but I have to go now," he said. "I have to find Miranda. I can't leave her hanging one more minute."

"I don't think that's going to be a problem. Look."

Behind Marcus, Mordant and Miranda had appeared at the top of the stairs. It was 5:00.

She stood for a moment and looked at both of us with a blank face. Mordant looked stunned, too.

In a flash, Miranda and Marcus headed toward each other. They met in the middle of the room and looked deeply in to each other's eyes. Marcus put his hands on Miranda's shoulders and said, "Baby, I have so much to tell you. But, the most important thing you need to know is that I love you. I love you more today than ever. You are the love of my life and I'm so sorry I hurt you."

And with that, Miranda started to cry – again. This time it was tears of joy. They embraced while Mordant quietly slipped by and came to the table to sit with me.

We respectfully turned our backs to the couple and began to exchange notes. I told him all about the hotel incident and how the nice women at the massage school took such good care of me. I explained the whole massage school secret exchange issue as well as the visitation from Miranda's father.

The barkeep brought the food Marcus ordered and I took it. Mordant told me about the bookstore, lunch, and his adventures with Miranda. Of course, he noticed that we had just witnessed, moments ago, the old "Their eyes met, their lips touched, and they just knew." We actually laughed.

We must have spoken for quite some time, because, at one point we noticed Marcus and Miranda were gone. By that time the food was cold but we were starving so we ate our cold Thai food and I sipped the lime juice, Hornitos™, and Sangrita. Together, my pal Mordant and I pondered the mysteries of the Universe.

Eventually, the sun set and the stars came out. The roof of The Roof Top was rolled back and the starry ceiling covered us. To our surprise, Marcus and Miranda came back and joined us. We sat and talked for quite some time as they shared stories about their Thai adventure and their plans to go back to LA and open a massage business.

Soon enough, Mordant and I suggested that they check out Tao Garden together. We explained meditation and Chi Kung and the importance of understanding Taoist Quantum Manifestation. The young couple said Tao Garden was a bit out of their way, but if the Universe pointed them in that direction they'd think about it. I think they were cosmic-experienced out.

Not at all to my surprise, within 15 minutes of speaking of Universal Tao, a group of students from Tao Garden, fresh from meditation with Master Chia, showed up at the Roof Top. To be fair, I knew all along that this was a popular hang out for Master Chia's students. The four of us just laughed at the ridiculousness of the whole thing. We were growing accustomed to the synchronicities now. Mordant says he heard Marcus tell one young Tao student that he and Miranda would love to come check out Tao Garden and that e-mail addresses were exchanged.

By evening's end, the group had pushed a few tables together and was sitting in a big circle on the floor, soaking up the experience like only foreign visitors can.

Mordant and I? We may have been moved around like pieces on a chess board, but ultimately, we remembered how to play the game and everybody won.

## THE WHINERS AND COMPLAINERS

**Good men are not argumentative.**
**The argumentative are not good.**

-Laozi

**WHINE[15] (whin)**
➢ To cry in or utter a high-pitched, long drawn-out plaintive sound
➢ to complain in a querulous or childish way
➢ a complaint - one that causes mild contempt

**COMPLAIN[16] (kom-plan)**
➢ to express dissatisfaction
➢ To express pin or distress

Similar to the bard of the Renaissance era, Whiners and Complainers will passionately express their grief as if they were reciting a song or a poem. Unlike the bard, however, Whiners and Complainers are about as entertaining as hemorrhoids. Whiners and Complainers will ride the horse even after it's dead. They will narrate for any unoccupied ear each disappointing detail of their pain-filled drama. Just for the record, the only difference between Whiners and Complainers and a Victim is that a Whiner and Complainer will verbalize their constant complaints while the

15 The New Lexicon Webster's Dictionary of the English Language 1988 Lexion Publications Inc. page 1121.

16 The New Lexicon Webster's Dictionary of the English Language 1988 Lexion Publications Inc. page 200.

Victim will internalize theirs. For healthy people, Whiners and Complainers inspire the same sort of reaction that scraping your fingernails on a chalkboard does. We have all experienced the way it feels when things don't turn out the way we planned. It sucks. Nevertheless, a healthy person is aware that "this, too, shall pass." Whiners and Complainers thrive on group negativity, so get ready to join in or tune out if you are going to date one.

The following are the most common reactions to being exposed to Whiners and Complainers for an extended period of time:

➢ Melting of the ears
➢ Involuntary clenching of the fists, jaw, and buttocks
➢ Desire to bear arms

## Why-oh-why would anyone date Whiners and Complainers?

Sarina here. Hate to say it, but Whiners and Complainers tend to date each other. They have to. The rest of us can't deal with it. I suppose they may find happiness in the arms of a Victim. Maybe a Victim would commiserate? As long as it takes the Whiner's attention off me, I don't care who comes along and takes this person away! I resemble that remark: Hard to accept that you are a Whiner and Complainer? Good. If the idea is unappealing to you, try these simple remedies:

➢ Never speak ill of a person unless they are in the room, participating in the conversation.
➢ There are 1,000 ways *not* to accomplish something. Give equal conversation time to discussing the one way you *can* accomplish something.

So, if you're not a Whiner and Complainer and you're not a Victim and you find yourself sitting across the dining table from a Whiner and Complainer, don't be surprised if your fork finds it's way into the back of your hand. That in itself should indicate it's time for the check; permanently.

### Sarina's addendum that Mordant does not subscribe to:

There is one exception: If your date is intensely attractive and you are intent on taking them home with you, a muzzle is an option. If you're willing to forego copulation or you're fresh out of muzzles, I have a couple of other ideas on how to deal with Whiners and Complainers

➢ Ear plugs
➢ Test the "Tree Falling in the Woods" theory. Find out if a Whiner

and Complainer complains and no one is there to hear it, does it actually make an annoying Whine

## But seriously folks . . .

As much as option two seems like a joke, often it is your only recourse. Some people just aren't happy unless there's something wrong. It's what they want. Believe it or not, they like their lives filled with grief. What's more, they expect their lives to be filled with grief. And guess what. They want you to grieve, too. These people are better left to their own devices. Train yourself to be attracted to joy and success. There is a very real danger in being intimately involved with Whiners and Complainers in that they may unknowingly drain you of your Chi.

Think about it. Haven't you ever hung out for a few hours with someone who's *really* down and out? Being a good friend, you spend your energy trying to help them see the lighter side of the issue. If you're not successful, how do you feel?

Another way to test this theory is to sit in at some sort of hate rally. Try it. After a few minutes of sitting in a room full of escalated, bitter Whiners and Complainers, close your eyes and experience your body. If you feel drained, shaky, or upset, pay attention! Even if you can handle it, ask yourself if this is really what you want.

One of the practices of the ancient Tao is the Sealing Of The Five Senses. Taoists believe that you may lose Chi by seeing, hearing, smelling, speaking or feeling excess negativity. Test it for yourself, but not for too long

**DO NOT SIT LONG WITH A SAD FRIEND.**
**WHEN IN THE GARDEN, DO YOU LOOK AT**
**ROSES OR THORNS?**
**SPEND MORE TIME WITH JASMINE AND**
**ROSES.**

Interpretation of a piece of poetry by Rumi

# THE ABUSERS

**Perhaps they too realize their dependence on the lowly.**

-**Laozi**

## ABUSE[17] (uh-byooz)

➢ to be used badly or wrongly
➢ to ill treat - injure
➢ to call foul names

It's like this . . .

If you're involved with a person who abuses drugs, alcohol, food, or any other substance, know now that this person is sick. To deny the problem is inappropriate and will be disappointing as well as potentially detrimental to their healing process. This is no joke and they (or you) need to get professional help.

If you are involved with a person that is verbally abusive you could try gluing their mouth shut while they sleep. However, we still recommend leaving the relationship until that person has received professional therapy and has demonstrated at least one year of successful behavior.

If you are involved with a person who is physically abusive, LEAVE. We don't get the chance to laugh at ourselves if we're dead.

---

17   The New Lexicon Webster's Dictionary of the English Language 1988 Lexion Publications Inc. page 4

# Hornitos™ Cranbarita
## (Or, if you make enough for your friends...)
## The Relief Pitcher

A creative twist on the original Margarita, the Cranbarita is sure to leave your taste buds tingling. Deliciously sweet with the perfect combination of sour.  A virtuoso in balance.

1 part Hornitos™ Reposado Tequila

1 1/2 parts sweet & sour

3/4 part cranberry juice

Rim the outside of a margarita glass with lime and dip into sugar. Add ice to the glass.  Fill a drink shaker with ice, tequila, sweet & sour, and cranberry juice. Shake and strain into margarita glass. Smile to your taste buds, take a sip, and appreciate.

drink smart

The highest form of goodness is like water.
Water knows how to benefit all
things without striving with them.
It stays in places loathed by all men.
Therefore, it comes near the Tao.

In choosing your dwelling, know
how to keep to the ground.
In cultivating your mind, know
how to dive in the hidden deeps.
In dealing with others, know
how to be gentle and kind.
In speaking, know how to keep your words.
In governing, know how to maintain order.
In transacting business,
know how to be efficient.
In making a move, know how to
choose the right moment.

If you do not strive with others,
You will be free from blame.

-Tao Te Ching

# Chapter 4

## WHAT TO DO

Mordant and I have helped you determine that you are the painter, your dates and loved ones are the canvas, and that you are indeed a powerful person because you and only you may manifest what you believe to be true. So what do you do if you are manifesting the uglies? First, find your local Universal Healing Tao Instructor and get Inner Smile and Six Healing Sounds instruction. Tell them Sarina sent you.

*And* . . .

I have compiled some of my favorite visualizations and mantras (chants) to help break the negative thinking patterns that are screwing up your life. Once you have memorized some of the chants, you may do them anywhere, including as you fall asleep, while the meditations require a controlled, quiet space to fully focus and achieve maximum benefits.

Begin by finding a quiet spot where no phones or other noises will distract you. To learn effectively, sit in a chair with your feet planted on the ground, your back straight, and your hands naturally placed on your lap. A good alternative is a comfy bathtub. Smile. Close your eyes. Relax. Smile some more and begin your practice.

# Visualization for Letting Someone Go

You must be sure you are finished suffering over this person. You must be 100% willing to breathe in the freedom of being detached from this individual.

### YOU MUST BE WILLING TO LET THEM GO.

You will know when it has worked for you because your obsession with the person you are focusing on will dissipate. Remember, you have to want to be happy more than you want to be connected to this person.

> ➢ Close your eyes and gently smile.
> ➢ If you are a Bible person, you may use the Lord's Prayer. When it speaks of forgiving for trespasses, forgive yourself and the person in question. Say this prayer one time. If you are not a Bible person, declare that you forgive yourself for your ill behavior and you forgive the other person for theirs. (You must do this even if you do not believe you have behaved poorly.)
> ➢ In your mind's eye, see this person as their highest, most enlightened self. See them dressed in white and standing in a cloud of pink mist. Pink symbolizes love.
> ➢ See this person smile at you.
> ➢ See this person turn around and walk away. Watch them as they disappear in to the pink mist of love.
> ➢ Know that they are walking away, to a better place, never to return

Do this every day for 90 days. The first day you forget to think about your ex, is the day you know your practice worked

It is amazing how many folks in pain, when given the choice, choose to stay with their pain instead of being freed from it. These folks ill refuse this meditation. They just aren't ready to let go of the one they used to love. Don't be too hard on yourself if you are one of these people. Get some counsel and try again when you are ready.

# Visualization for Loving Your Body

It is important that we feel beautiful inside and out. Don't kid yourself that those few extra pounds or the skinny knees are the reason you strike out in the romance department. We know too much to buy into that crap.You must build the strong foundation of self-love in order to manifest a sweetie who feels the same way. Try this next meditation and see what happens in 30 days when you look in the mirror.

- ଓ Close your eyes and gently smile.

- ଓ See a picture of yourself in your mind's eye. See this version of you floating above you. You are naked.

- ଓ See the front of your body.

- ଓ Now, focus on your head. See your hair, eyes, skin, nose, and mouth. See them morph into the perfect you. See your beautiful eyes as they captivate even you. Closely examine every inch of your head and face until it becomes what you are satisfied with.

- ଓ Next, move your inner vision to your throat, shoulders, and arms. See the throat as sleek and healthy. See your shoulders and arms as healthy and sexy.

- ଓ Next, see your chest, waist, and belly. What is your heart's desire? Thin? Plump? Muscular? See yourself as the healthiest version of yourself.

- ଓ Next, incorporate your hips, groin, and legs. Don't miss anything. Spend a little time getting to know every inch of your beautiful, healthy body. What does your skin look and feel like?

- ଓ Now, rotate the image of your body and see the back of your head, neck, shoulders, and arms. See the back of your head and upper body as the most perfect version of yourself. View the muscles and skin as the image of graceful beauty.

- ଓ Focus on your waist, back and buttocks. What is your heart's desire? Thin? Plump? Muscular? What does your skin look and feel like? Again, see yourself as the healthiest version of yourself

- ଓ Incorporate your legs. Don't miss anything. Spend a little time getting to know every inch of your beautiful, healthy body.

- ଓ When you are finished, see the perfect, healthy person above you in its entirety.

- ଓ Very slowly, watch as this image begins to get very small – about the size of a spool of thread. Allow this small image to become a white, glowing star about six inches above your head.

- ଓ Allow the glowing white color to enter your body through your crown (the top of your head). Feel how this color spreads to all areas of your body and effects every cell.

- ଓ Be aware that this white energy is changing your body and its energetic system.

- ଓ Smile.

- ଓ Rest.

## Do this every day for 60 to 120 days.

# Visualization for Creating a Partner

If you feel you are ready for intimacy, you may see yourself with your partner and begin manifesting a loving, healthy relationship. If you are not ready for intimacy, the following practice will dredge up those beliefs that stand between you and your goal. Be prepared to face them and commit to transforming your negative beliefs into positive ones. When you are ready, you may use this same practice to manifest a healthy partner.

Warning: If you are not currently engaged or in a committed relationship and would like to manifest one, you must not attempt to call a specific individual to you with this practice. Follow the Cardinal rule: never put a face on it. Let me repeat, *never put a face on it*. Once you do, your visualization becomes a manipulation. The price for energetically manipulating the thoughts of another person is the loss of that person. I'm warning you here and now, if you misuse or abuse this meditation, you may get your wish for a short period, but you will ultimately create loss and negativity.

If you are single and would like to use this meditation to create a new relationship, you must start from scratch. If you end up with someone you already know, that's just fine. You must trust in the process. Be content with being happy.

We do not use our imagery to manipulate Chi where we are not welcome. There are times when we have permission to co-create an outcome with a specific individual (assisting in healing an ailment is a good example). This is not one of those situations.

In this instance, we are co-creating a new reality with the Universe. That being said, it is appropriate to see a certain body type. Have a party on that one!

- ❧ Close your eyes and gently smile.

- ❧ Relax your body 100%.

- ❧ Take your awareness far, far above you and find a spiraling galaxy. Feel the centrifugal force of this spiraling galaxy. Where the mind goes, the Chi flows. Know that a piece of your energetic Self is out in the Universe watching this spiral.

- ❧ As you look closely at the center of this spiral, you will begin to notice something round in the center of it.

- ❧ The closer you look, the more you see that there is a round, clear bubble in the center of the vortex.

- ❧ Looking even closer, you see that there is a large, white, empty room in this bubble.

94

∝ Project an image of yourself in this room.

∝ Search your mind and find your ideal Sunday morning in your ideal home with your ideal sweetheart. Remember, don't put a face on it.

∝ Where is this house? What does it look like outside? Is there a car outside? What room are you in? What do the other rooms look like? What is in the kitchen? Do you drink coffee or tea on Sunday morning? What are you two doing? How are the two of you dressed? Are there children in the house?

∝ Who are you in the presence of this person? How do you feel? Are you financially free? Are you emotionally open? How does your life feel? How does your body feel? Again, what are you doing?

∝ Sit in this space for a while and get a strong feeling for who you are and how you feel on this ideal Sunday morning with your ideal partner in your ideal home.

∝ Smile to this vision.

∝ When you're ready, begin to pull your vision away from this room. See that it is inside the bubble, inside the spiraling galaxy.

∝ Next, watch as the stars in this galaxy begin to spiral around the bubble. Very soon, they create a cocoon of sparkling stars around the vision inside the bubble. You know it's in there, but you cannot see it.

∝ As you watch this cocoon, it begins to slowly drop down toward you.

∝ As the sparkling cocoon approaches, it gets smaller and smaller, until it reaches the crown of your head. It is the size of a spool of thread.

∝ Allow the cocoon to enter your head through the crown.

∝ You notice now that there is a spiraling galaxy in the top of your skull (the crown). Place the cocoon, with your vision inside of it, in the center of the spiraling galaxy.

∝ Smile to this spiraling galaxy and allow the energy of your vision to multiply.

∝ Move the cocoon to your throat. See that there is a spiraling galaxy in your throat. Place the cocoon in the center of this galaxy and allow this spiraling to clear any stuck Chi in your throat. This will allow you to speak freely on this subject.

∝ Smile to your throat.

∝ Move the cocoon to your heart. See the spiraling galaxy in the center of your torso at the level of the heart. Place the cocoon in the center of this galaxy. Allow the spiraling action to open your hear.

∝ Smile to your heart.

∝ Move the cocoon to your navel. See the spiraling galaxy in the center of your belly. Place the cocoon in the center of this galaxy.

∝ The navel is where we will store our cocooned vision. Leave the spiraling galaxy right where it is. See the white color radiate out from your belly and affect all the cells of your body.

∝ Smile to your navel. Smile to your vision.

∝ Rest.

Practice this meditation every day until you have the desired results.

## Healthy Romantic Declarations

A declaration is a public verbalization of a stand. In this case, we have supplied you with affirmative statements regarding the subject of romance. The more you say them, the more your brain will embrace them and the more real they will become.

Here are a few you may say out loud or sub-vocalize throughout the day:

**I am worthy of love.**
**I am an open, trusting person.**
**Love is safe and fun.**
**I am a magnet for a healthy partner.**
**I am comfortable with intimacy.**
**I will recognize healthy partners**
**when I see them.**

# Chapter 5

## VARIATIONS ON A THEME

**From Sarina:**

First, it occurred to me that women are not the only ones who enter into relationships with men. Men do, too. What happens when fire meets fire (Yang meets Yang)?

We would be remiss if we neglected to acknowledge our brothers in dating combat. Although this book appears to be written for ladies, when reading the contributions from our male friends who are intimate with men, we see clearly that people are people, regardless of their sexual preference. Mordant concurred that this subject should be included in this reading.

We asked our friend Steven, a man who has been in an intimate and committed relationship for over 14 years as of the time if this writing, for insight into the world of Yang/Yang (male/male) relationships. Interestingly enough, his response applies to Yin/Yang (female/male) relationships as well. He is our voice of experience and maturity.

We will also hear from Eric, a young man who also dates men and offers insights into the issues he faces. I am proud to say Eric has studied with both Mordant and I, is an avid lover of the Tao, and we believe it shows in his insights.

Next, no text on intimacy would be complete without mentioning Yin/Yin (female/female) relationships. Mordant conducted a one-on-one interview with a lady friend to get some insight. We have included the results of that most charming interview here as well.

Lastly, same-sex relations are not the only unique form of intimacy we wanted to touch upon briefly. We have two gals – both over 60 – who have a little something to say. One, a woman who is deeply involved in her May/December relationship, and one who chooses to remain single. We hope you enjoy their humor and candor as much as we do

## Steven's Insights:

Sarina asked if gay relationships are different from straight ones. I can only answer that in many ways they are and in many ways are not. Two people in a relationship, be it straight or gay, are going to expose their issues no matter what the sexual preference. In my opinion, the right partner will help you (if you're willing) to work out life's lessons. You are here to learn and if you're open to this, it can be a wonderful journey.

Early on in my coming out, I used to think that I could avoid all those man/woman difficulties and live happily ever after with great sex and perfect understanding. After all, I was subtracting the "war of the sexes" wasn't I? Unfortunately, after some failed relationships, I learned that I could re-create my parent's imperfect rapport...with a man. Oh, lucky me.

I feel strongly that with mature relationships, gay or straight, we are seeking companionship most of all. Don't get me wrong, sex is great. It is an integral part of intimacy, but if something happens such as illness, it's comforting to know that your partner would be there just to talk to or be quiet together. We seek the Tao of Intimacy on many important levels: emotional, intellectual, as well as physical. I cannot tell you how many times myself or friends of mine have flung themselves into a "relationship" because the sex was so good the other needs were ignored. Of course, when it fell apart we blamed the other person. Funny when you see it spelled out that way.

When asked to write how I have maintained a Yang/Yang, 14+/-year relationship, I had to take time to sort out what my personal "keys" were.

1) First and foremost is accepting my partner for who he is (including his shortcomings). This was tough to learn, but crucial.

"I get to be happy!" I say it over and over, especially when I find myself blaming my sweetheart for my poor state of mind. In the beginning, it was common for me to blame my darling. "He is such a lazy slob! Why doesn't he do something around here instead of just watch TV?" Negative thoughts only worked me into frenzy and led to a dirty fight. Now, with reminding myself to accept him for who he is and communicate my wishes to him (even if I don't want to), the outcome is usually productive and negates the need for cheap drama.

2) Communication – a must. No one is a mind reader; don't expect him or her to be. I learned to ask for what I need and want in the clearest language I could muster. I learned to be direct. Now, if I am unhappy, I say so, and if I'm happy, I let him in on my good mood.

If you don't have good communication skills, find a counselor who can help. Do it for both of you! It will help with all your dealings and relationships – not just the intimate ones.

For example, I was brought up to prepare for entertaining by having a well planned out "Martha week." There was no last minute rush. My mother took it to the extreme; the week bled right into the party and she never really stopped to enjoy the fun.

So this is the way I thought it should be: In comes my partner (we will call him "Last Minute Manny"). Everything gets put off till the day of the party, and then you run around cleaning (I use that term loosely) and cooking, setting the table, etc. By party time, you're ready to crash. So you can see why this would make me just a little testy.

First, I used to do it all myself, in the days before the event. I got the joy of being a martyr and resentful. My sweetheart knew that there would be a blow up after the party every time, but he never knew why *until I told him*. He was amazed that I expected him to psychically ferret out what was wrong with me. Then he told me that as long as the company is wonderful, he could not care less about the setting. Wow.

So how did holding my feelings back serve me? I got to be pissed off and feel like a servant. After some soul searching, I discovered that perfection seeking (or façade) was a way to hide my feelings of not being good enough. I wasn't enough and therefore had to make other things "perfect" to hide my lacking. All this I pushed onto my partner, Last Minute Manny.

In a move of self-preservation and improved mental health, I decided that if my friends are going to judge me by my "extreme cleanliness standard," then they are not the positive support I need. I decided resenting my partner every time we had company was silly. Now, I do some of the work ahead of time, and if it doesn't get done, oh well. Not that the old voices don't shout once in a while, but I remind myself constantly that the people coming to see us are doing just that, and if the house is not Martha perfect, it's OK.

3) No more negative parental re-enactments. Folks, if you're an adult you can't blame your parents any more.

My parents taught me that others need to change, not me; but we never share what the changes need to be. They showed me that you stuff what feelings you have till you and your partner have a screaming match. I was taught that this is what couples do and that this is *love*. Boy, was I confused when I grew up to be a man who certainly did not want constant blow-ups in his relationship!

As an adult, I am responsible for my reality, so I choose to monitor angry feelings and fights by taking time to think. I catch myself and say to my partner, "I can't talk to you right now. I will just pick a fight and say hurtful things." That gives me time to figure out what my feelings are and if this is worth debate.

I have also found it useful to remember that, male or female, many of us choose partners who help us heal unresolved issues with our parents. Gay or straight, most of us do it. Volumes have been written in the subject and it's still a huge issue for many of us. When my partner and I first got together, I don't know how many times I said to myself, "He is acting just like my dad." Then I realized I was acting like my mother! All I needed was the Betty Crocker frock. The good news is that once you have this awareness, it makes a vast amount of difference, and the opportunity for healing presents itself.

4) Work on yourself. Do it for you! If you're happy and growing, then this will show up in your relationship. Sure, there is the fear that you may outgrow your partner, and vice versa. It may happen, but if you talk to your partner about your growth and concerns, you may get lucky and grow together.

As I made changes, things got easier. For example, my partner recently got a bad cold and moped around the house doing nothing but messing it up and seeking sympathy. In the beginning, I was all Florence Nightingale (which is my training, not my desire). But by the end of the illness, I was feeling a bit more Dr. Kevorkian. The old me was fighting the new. Would he love me even if I don't care take him? As love would have it, he adapted. (Remember, don't expect your partner to change, but be supportive if change for the better occurs.)

Those are my four keys to successful partnering. We all have ways of doing things, but having a partner means that you don't always get to do it that way. You have to adapt; you have to grow. You could spend the rest of your life being angry and frustrated, or you can find a middle ground. Again, the choice is yours.

## Steven's Quote:

When asked, "How have you two stayed together for so long?" my answer is:

**"Well, in the first few years I used to try the pillow over the face, but he is stronger than I, so he kept getting free. I took that to mean we were supposed to be together!"**

## Eric Thurnbeck answers the question: "What About Men Who Date Men?"

Having discussed the theories about the control we have over manifesting our own reality (as taught both by Quantum Manifestation and the Tao), it's easy to see that our beliefs can, and will, affect the lives we lead. That being said, it's also easy to recognize that even the *concept* of men dating men carries with it a lot of baggage, in both the gay and straight communities. Consider for a moment the archetypes of gay men that exist in popular culture. These men are impeccably dressed, stylish, narcissistic, handsome, prone to histrionic behavior, and have lists of sexual conquests that read like tax audit receipts. These characters are involved in continuous drama of their own making, have unstable relationships, and suffer the constant pressure to be young, beautiful, and thin. Whether the stereotype in question is a hulking gym-bunny in a jockstrap or a wilting, effeminate hairdresser wearing pastels, they all have something in common: they like to screw as much as possible, and they like to get noticed.

The other widespread belief to consider is that gay people are, in general, disliked and misunderstood by many others. Even in the days of the Fab Five and *Will & Grace*, being gay is, in many parts of the world, still a controversy.

These beliefs teach gay men to manifest the wrong things. From an early age, we're taught certain truths about being gay: that our relationships are temporary and unstable (so unstable, in fact, that they cannot be recognized by law in the United States), that we are sexually promiscuous (well, okay, many of us are), and that we will lead lives of fear and persecution.

If we *believe*, deep in our hearts, that we will never find true love because all men are pigs, well, guess what – that's exactly what will happen. We will sabotage our chances at happiness because we buy into the hype that "Mr. Right Now" *is all we get*. We'll have nothing but exclusively physical relationships. We'll date head-cases who don't know themselves. And we'll all bemoan our fates, wishing we could be rescued by Prince Charming, but knowing deep down, that he moved in with Mr. Right a long-ass time ago.

The good news is this: if we can get over ourselves and stop whining about how shallow gay relationships are, *we can build something of meaning and substance.*

## The Cultural Enactment of the Gay Myth

When I was a teenager, I was deeply unhappy. In addition to all the angst one would expect a teenager to experience, I suffered from clinical depression (though I would not be officially diagnosed until I was 23). I also harbored a burning secret that I was different. I grew up in a small town, where being gay was simply not considered a viable option. The majority of my peers treated me poorly or indifferently, as my strangeness was quite apparent to anyone who looked.

I felt persecuted. I was viewed with suspicion because I was different, and as I grew up, I heard many hateful words used to describe gay people. I became intimate with the emotions of *hatred* and *cruelty*, both directly and indirectly. I internalized not only the rough treatment I received growing up, but also the general animosity that was expressed towards homosexuals. I know now that I wasn't alone.

While our society has made strides in overcoming the prejudices about gays, we all understand that there's a long way to go. It's great to see gay characters on primetime TV, but any of us who have had to think twice about stopping at certain gas stations at night know not to kid ourselves – homophobia is not entirely a thing of the past.

In accordance with what I have learned about Taoist philosophy, I believe homophobia is one of the major obstacles that gay men have in building functional relationships. The Taoist Chi Kung teaches us that we carry certain emotions in certain organs of the body. Each organ stores both positive and negative energies, which are expressed as constructive and destructive emotions. The heart is the seat of love, but also *hatred* and *cruelty*. If we internalize too much of the latter, expressing the former becomes very difficult

An unfortunate side effect of this dynamic is that gay men often re-create the rejection of their youth within their adult relationships. I've known plenty of guys who found themselves pushing their boyfriends away for reasons inexplicable to them. When I offered advice through tarot readings, I found the same thing playing itself out over and over: Rejection was something these men were comfortable with, while intimacy was not. They knew how to navigate rejection since they'd been familiar with it for years. Acceptance, on the other hand, was something new – it presented these men with something they had never before faced and weren't equipped to handle. The result of this deficiency was that they placed distance between themselves and the men who loved them, actually *creating* the abandonment they were afraid of experiencing all over again. This only feeds into the cycle of self-loathing that many gay men become trapped in, which is constantly reinforced by the messages we receive from society.

When you have millions of people all over the world targeting one group with all that negative energy, is it any wonder why gay men can be such bitches? Another way these patterns can manifest is when the negative emotions we are subjected to become internalized to such a degree that we begin to emulate figures who personify those emotions. Anyone familiar with gay subculture or has read a personal ad in a gay publication has seen it: Guys looking for "straight-acting only" men to share their beds with; adopting the same homophobic judgments to which they were subjected in their earlier years. Another obvious clue is the obsession with youth that is so deeply engrained into the gay dating ritual: men invariably grow older as time passes, but very often the "type" they search for as a potential mate remains static. These men continue to search for twenty-something (or younger) guys, even as they enter their thirties, forties, and fifties. Are these men seeking out others who embody the masculine youth to which they aspired (and perhaps failed to reach) attempting to correct the rejections they experienced in the past? If these men can find the straight-acting, masculine, muscular, twenty-five-year-old mate, do they believe that the pain of their pasts will disappear?

It's a tempting theory. After all, who *wouldn't* want to bed the above-mentioned hottie anyway? And if doing so offers up a clear slate, so much the better, right? The only flaw in this idea is that none of us can hope for an external force to alter our internal emotional and energetic chemistry. This change has to be wrought from the inside out (though having a man change another man from the inside is, to say the least, intriguing).

In all seriousness, the only way for us to manifest the love we desire is to make room for it. We have to balance out the hatred we've experienced (and expressed) with love. With balanced hearts, we can make ourselves open to unconditional love. If our hearts are filled with hatred and cruelty, we can't expect to receive much of anything else.

Towards that goal, we need to think twice about what we feel and how we express those feelings. Look at all the kinds of love in your life– friendly, familial, and romantic. Do those relationships have strings attached? Are they toxic? Do they carry the weight of inappropriate obligation?

We also need to seriously consider how we behave in our day-to-day lives. Examining your own behavior, do you find that you make more cruel or loving comments? Do you welcome new people into your life with openness or reservation? Are you quick to judge? Do you carry your own prejudices? Do you love more people than you hate? If *hatred* and *cruelty* rule your heart, that's something you need to get over before *love* will find its way into your life.

## Manifesting Heaven and Hell

These theories sound great on paper, but how do they apply to real life? While I've cited the experiences of others in the preceding paragraphs, I'd be remiss not to write about how these concepts have affected my own life.

I've already described the unhappiness I experienced earlier in life. It was during this dark period that I first learned how to consciously manifest the things I desired. Unfortunately, I learned to manifest all the wrong things before I realized I could be genuinely happy.

When I was nineteen, I desired a mate. After losing my virginity to a man who was, shall we say, less than ideal, I sought out an attachment of greater stability – one not based entirely on sexual attraction, but also mutual interests and a general caring for one another's well-being. I crafted an old-fashioned love charm, picturing the man I wanted in my mind, even down to the color of his eyes: like the sea and the sky, I remember. My final criterion was this: *He needed to love me as much as I wanted to love him*

You can probably see where this is going.

I *wanted* to love someone with all my being. I wanted a whirlwind, Hollywood romance (*sans* tragic ending). When he arrived a few months later I was stunned – I'd even gotten the eye color right; he was muscular, polite, and soft-spoken. He was a patient tutor, educating me in the arts of both sex and relationships, attempting to draw out my better qualities, to learn my secrets.

I was interested in him, but I didn't love him, not really. I was young. I wouldn't have known a good man if he bit me on the ass. My emotions were chaotic and destructive, and he always regarded me with the same gentleness and patience, which was maddening. Ultimately, I pushed him away, citing my reasons as follows: *I'm not sure what love feels like, but I don't think it feels like indifference.* But he loved me as much as I wanted to love him, and while I didn't break his heart, I know I bruised it a bit. Fortunately, he is a resilient man and we remain friends to this day.

My second experience in manifestation was far less innocuous. When I was 23, I suffered an emotional break as a result of undiagnosed clinical depression. I woke my parents at 1 A.M. and told them that if I wasn't taken to a hospital immediately, I would do myself serious harm. I was hospitalized for five days, underwent a clinical analysis, and put on a prescription and psychotherapeutic regimen.

Ultimately, it was the best thing that could have happened. I shudder to think what could have taken place if I hadn't had the courage to ask for help.

About two months after being released, I decided to go out alone. I went to a club, smoked, and danced. I wanted to be found beautiful, but my self-esteem had taken a fatal blow, and I was certain I would devastate anyone unlucky enough to succumb to my siren song.

But someone found me. Ironically enough, it was his birthday. He told me I was beautiful. We danced, we talked, and he bought me drinks. I made his friends laugh with my dark humor. He was enthralled. How could I resist the opportunity to have my ego stroked, to restore my self-image?

We began dating, but within a week or so, his true nature began to show through the cracks in his armor – his addictions, his self-defeating thoughts, and his bulimia. He was just barely holding it together, and when he told me that he had planned to kill himself the night we met, but that I'd changed his mind, I knew I was in over my head. My friends were gracious for the most part, but they all issued warnings I had no desire to heed – he was too much for me, too soon, that it wasn't my responsibility to rescue him from himself.

I was frightened by what might happen if I left him so I remained, growing more and more certain with each day that this romance could only end in disaster. His condition deteriorated, until he was finally taken by ambulance from his office to a behavioral health center and hospitalized. His experience mirrored my own, almost exactly. He was evaluated, placed on medication, and ordered to see a therapist.

Shortly afterward, I ended the relationship. I knew we could only drag one another down with our terrible gravity, that we would only reinforce one another's weaknesses. He acquiesced, telling me he could never hold onto me if he knew I wanted to leave. We talked, cried, and hugged, vowing to help one another as friends.

I came to learn some time later that immediately after I left, he cut his wrists and attempted to overdose on his medication. Fortunately, he survived and ultimately recovered. But I could never escape wondering why he had chosen *me*, of all the people in that crowded, smoky bar that night.

Of course, the answer is self-evident: I was the one who chose him, as he embodied all of the things I feared about myself at the time.

My most recent experience in manifesting my fears took years to overcome. I met him at the same bar where I'd met my previous boyfriend (you'd think I'd have learned, right?). Our relationship began well enough, though his behavior was somewhat simplistic and juvenile. Against my better judgment, I went to work for him, as he owned his own business. Things went well at first. He was (very) attentive, sweet, and constant. He was also overemotional, unpredictable, and had relationship issues of his own. I soon learned he had an unflushable ex, an overbearing mother, and a general touchy interaction with the human race.

In retrospect, I should have seen the signs. His temper would flare at odd moments, followed by bouts of neediness and grief. None of my friends really liked him, which sparked an unending conflict about nine months into the relationship.

Despite my best attempts to bury the issue, his behavior spiraled out of control, inciting him to send endless scathing emails to my friends calling them blistering names and doing anything he could to rile them. I warned him repeatedly to cease and desist, but he never did.

Ultimately, I had to make good my threats to leave, which broke my heart. For a while, I'd really kidded myself into believing that he could be the one who would offer me stability and a place to belong.

But therein lay the rub.

In my search for someone to accept me and offer me safety, I manifested a man who felt so empty inside that he sought validation from everyone he met, and when he didn't get it he reacted in hatred and violence. It took over two years for the ugly emails to stop, and only then because I'd obtained an injunction from the police.

It was only then that I learned that *no man would ever make me happy*. My objective shifted. Instead of seeking happiness from without, I decided to find contentment within and then *create* happiness with another person.

It took years for me to even consider the idea of trusting another man. I tomcatted around seeking amusement in the beds of strangers, exploring the more extreme sides of my desire. After long months spent with nameless men, I began to want something more. I wanted a man who respected himself, who knew himself well, and could match me both intellectually and emotionally. I wanted someone with my sex drive and my appreciation for the esoteric. I wanted a lover who could draw out my better qualities instead of my weaknesses. I think I may have found him.

He's not perfect, not by any means – I can see many of my own fears in him still, especially my fear of betrayal. He is not quite secure with himself, but he is aware of his own issues and is dedicated to overcoming them. In the plus column, he is kind, funny, and open; he calls me on my bullshit and has no problem demonstrating his affection. He loves the complexity of my mind, and he has a healthy sense of self-respect. The fact that he's lovely to look at and *delightful* to hold is a bonus

For the record, the sex is the best I've ever had, bar none.

While I'm not quite sure if this is "Happily Ever After," I'm wise enough to know that this is "Heaven on Earth"... and that I will savor the experience for as long as it lasts.

## Yin/Yin Relationships
## By R. Mordant Mahon

I was asked to interview a woman who is in a Yin/Yin relationship and chose my friend Dana She is a trained actor who performs at Renaissance Festivals across the United States. Though she calls herself an entertainer, she prefers the term "new vaudevillian." Dana has been in both heterosexual and lesbian relationships. The following are excerpts from a conversation we had. I took a little artistic license, but for the most part, this is what she said:

**Have you had romantic experience with both genders?**
I have; but honestly, I'd have to say that my mature relationships have been with women.

**According to the Tao, Women are considered Yin (Fire wrapped in Water), and Men are considered Yang (Water wrapped in Fire). Tell us something about being in a Yin/Yin relationship. Where do you figure into the elemental chart, Dana?**
Anything doubled, you get double the flavor, double the good, but you also get double the complexity of that kind of being.

I hate to generalize, but women tend to communicate more. Culturally we've been handed that card. So, it's reinforced that we're allowed to be emotional. Therefore, the level of intimacy with women tends to be higher. Men in our culture aren't allowed that. Quite often, I feel like men got the raw end of the deal. Anyhow, if you have two women that have identified with that cultural baggage or biological tendencies – whichever you believe to be true – then you double the emotion. If you double the emotion, it can be more to wade through.

Those are stereotypes to be sure. But, if we're going to use labels, on the spectrum of masculinity and femininity I think I'm sort of in the middle if not leaning toward the stereotypical feminine. There are women who identify more with masculinity than femininity, and there are men who identify with femininity more than masculinity. It's a really tricky subject.

**What is something classically beautiful about Yin/Yin relationships?**

There is a soft, cuddly side to women I love. In my relationships, the intimacy level of a woman seems to be higher than most men I've dated. For example, many women can enjoy a night of just cuddling, and that's *perfect*, that's all it needs to be. Both partners can be satisfied with that. I think that exists to a greater extent with women than it does with men.

**Could you tell us one pitfall of a Yin/Yin relationship?**

This same cuddling can lead, stereotypically, to something called *Bed Death*. Because they get *so* cuddly and *so* friendly that eventually, they stop having sex. They wake up one day and say, "Wait a minute. What happened to our sex life?"

**Our friend Eric wrote extensively on society and the effects of cultural judgments on same-sex romance. Do you think society's reaction to lesbians matters in a relationship?**

It can. But one of the truths around is realizing the baggage you've been handed was *handed* to you. We choose to hang onto that baggage or to let it go. That's an individual thing. Don't you think that exists for every human being?

**As a human being, do you think you've grown more as a lesbian? Would a heterosexual relationship have offered you the same opportunities?**

Again, a tricky subject. On one hand, as a woman, there are the stereotypical Yin/Yin communication opportunities I spoke of earlier. Then add the awareness that comes from processing the fact that we're different. Recognizing that difference tends to put gay people in touch with their feelings earlier in life. For us, there's something that isn't on the normal "worksheet." I think we might be nudged a little harder toward self-awareness because we *have to* figure some things out on our own.

On the other hand, when relating to people across the board, you're going to find similar issues. Ultimately, it's going to boil down to two humans coming together and learning from each other. I can't remember who said this, but, "relationships aren't here to make us happy; relationships are here to teach us things." Dealing with idiosyncrasies in the people I love can be an opportunity for personal growth. As I said before, it's more of a human thing than a lesbian thing.

Being gay or straight is not a ticket to self-awareness. Personally, I came out late. I didn't get it until I was about 23. The funny thing is, when I called my best friend to give her the big news, she said, "Uh...yeah." I was like, "Excuse me!? You mean you've known all this time?" She said, "Well, it's not the kind of thing that you tell somebody. They have to figure it out on their own."

Can you give us a finishing thought...about love?

I really think you have to love yourself first. If you're looking for another person to *finish* you, the relationship is definitely limping, if not crippled. I don't believe two people come together to finish each other. I believe you create something together, but I don't think that it's half you and half that person. I think it's a whole you and a whole other person coming together to create something entirely separate. So, I believe learning to be compassionate, caring, supportive, and loving towards yourself will make you compassionate, caring, and supportive toward your mate and to humanity in general.

There is a Celtic Rune with a message identical to Dana's parting thought. Interestingly enough, it is the Rune of Partnership. To paraphrase, it says that a healthy relationship is the by-product of two separate, but whole beings that come together and form a third entity called "us."

## Rosie's Dating After 60 (Or Do I Really Want to Do That?)

So I thought it would be fun to contribute a chapter to this book until I actually sat down to do it. I had all these hilarious thoughts going through my mind. I couldn't wait to pen those passages, and now it's time.

Perfect, I can't remember anything I thought was so funny. So let's start with that. After all, dating requires a good memory when you're postmenopausal – especially if you lie about your age, your sex drive, your social security status, your medications, your exercise habits, your digestion, your incontinence, the kind of music you like, your need to eat dinner no later than 6 p.m. and the list goes on.

Oh, for the simpler days when the only things I could think about were my weight, my make-up, my hair, my cleavage, and my body odors. I still have those concerns but they come after the former concerns. So by the time I go through the entire list, I'm too tired to care if I ever meet "Mister Right" again!!

In my hormonal days, Mr. Right had to look good, smell good, and kiss well. Then my sex drive would follow him anywhere (and drag me along with it). Nowadays I have to consciously think about every aspect of "keeping company" with a man. I can't just go on autopilot and let my base instincts take over. I actually have to pay attention and choose the person. It sounds like so much work, so much energy.

Do I even care? Being a result-driven person, I got very modern and joined the electronic age.

I went online and signed up with an online dating community. I meticulously answered every question. I even had my daughter-in-law cheer me on as I felt like I was running a marathon. We definitely had a difference of opinion when it came to answering those questions. So we duked it out and in the end, she won. After a while, I hoped the computer would crash and I could go to bed. No luck! I had to suck it up and finish the whole damn thing.

The part I hated the most was the section on "Exercise." How humiliating! My idea of a good workout is vacuuming every inch of the house and using the crevice tool in every room. I work up a good sweat, and in the end, my house is clean! That doesn't happen at the gym.

Still, there was nothing about vacuuming on the application. There were questions about tennis, golf, running, swimming, biking, kayaking, hiking, jogging, aerobics, kickboxing, etc., but no vacuuming. God, I felt ancient and out of place. Then they want to know the frequency of exercise. Gads! The frequency? I vacuum once a week and spend the rest of the week recovering. Actually, it only takes me three days to recover. Not bad.

O.K. So I finish the application and they let me know that for a whole week I can use the service at no charge. Fantastic!! So I push the match button and I thought I heard a drum roll.

After two hours of telling the truth, there were "0" matches. It's two weeks later and it's still "0" matches.

Now I'm thinking about what's really important about dating at this stage of life. I hate to admit it but companionship seems to be what's missing. Yikes! Companionship? That's what dogs are for. So just the thought of dating after 60 is exhausting. I think I'll go to bed. Tomorrow's another day.

Rosie may have thrown in the towel, but our other friend over 60, who chooses a hysterical nom de plume, has jumped in the dating pool and finds the water to be worth the swim.

## May to December Romance
## By Dorothy Gayle

> **She:** Born 1943, Divorced, one son in college
>
> **He:** Born 1965, Single, no children

## January 27, 1990

On a lazy Saturday afternoon, she made a pot of coffee, opened a fresh pack of cigarettes, sat down at her kitchen table, and began to read the personals ads for amusement and for lack of nothing better to do. "How dull these people are," she thought to herself. As she was about to end this tedious exercise, there it was...a small ad that caught her eye. "25-year-old attractive musician seeks worldly woman." The word "worldly" intrigued her since it has so many different definitions. Without hesitation, she called the voicemail number in the ad and left a message. "I'm intrigued by your ad and would like to know your definition of 'worldly.' I also have a few surprises for you."

# Hornitos™ Sweet and Sour
## or as Sarina likes to call it
## the Yin & Yang

A refreshing cocktail with a split personality, smooth Hornitos™ vs. bitter cranberry, sweet syrup vs. the sour fruit juice.

It shouldn't work, but it assuredly does. This is the bittersweet symphony in a glass.

1 part Hornitos™ Reposado Tequila
1 ½ parts cranberry juice
Splash grenadine
Splash Club Soda

Fill a rocks glass with ice, then pour tequila and cranberry juice over the rocks. Add a splash of grenadine, stir – and be stirred.

drink 🙂 smart

# Chapter 6

## EPILOGUE

After days of staring at a blank screen, making every effort to write the Epilogue for this book, I finally have two thoughts that are worth sharing:

1) Intimacy isn't that complicated; *you are*. We each have *this* life and *this* body, once. Don't waste it. You choose your partners and you choose to stay if things go right or wrong. Know that we all have imperfections and those imperfections make us beautiful – even you. If one of your imperfections is that you can't stop buying into negative thoughts, get help. Talk to a therapist, try hypnosis, read healthy books, take a class, speak with healthy people, write a stand-up comedy routine about your love life and perform it for your friends – just frickin' do something to get your heart and mind open and positive!

2) Where the mind goes, the Chi flows. When you understand that *your world* is a reflection of *your beliefs*, the responsibility for success, or lack of it, rests squarely on your shoulders. Believe in miracles today and see what magic you create tomorrow.

Honestly, folks, it's just that simple.


Yours in the Tao,


Sarina Stone

# Bonus Chapter

## STAYING CLEAN IN A DIRTY BUSINESS

(The fine art of walking straight on the crooked path)

Comments, quips, suggestions, and bitches from friends and colleagues.

I'm throwing in, as a bonus, what could have ended up on the cutting room floor. It seemed a shame not to share some of this material just because it was not necessary to the main body of this book.

The following are a few anecdotes about what it is to be human. Some really brave men and women have contributed these. I want to take this opportunity to thank them.

Thanks a lot, guys.

**THE SAVIOR**
There he was,
warrior,
worshipper,
And she was . . .
released.
And after she rested,
basking in his strength,
she gathered her rescources,
built a new prison,
kissed him on the cheek,
and entered.

**–Sarina–**

## IT'S A GUY THING

Add these to the great mysteries of the world, because I'd really like to know.

⇨    Why is it that women like to bring up deeply intense issues at 3:00 a.m.?

⇨    Why is it that while she will lie awake in anguish all night, he will slumber in undeserved peace?

⇨    Why is it that after a long night of torture, she will look like death warmed over while he is chipper and refreshed?

## THE SIX MEN PER YEAR THEORY

I need to date about six men per year. Men are so alluring to me because they are, all at once, strong and romantic. Guys are great. There's nothing like being pursued by an intelligent, strong-minded Romeo to make a woman feel like the reigning goddess of light and beauty. I love that stuff.

Of course, I won't show a man right away how impressed I am. That's *my* job. *His* job is to wine and dine me and spend all of his money on me. *My* job is to act as if I get this kind of treatment all the time. Furthermore, I will relay to him that what I'm really looking for is a man who is not afraid to cry. These are the *job descriptions. For about two months*. Then things change dramatically.

Once the glitter fades, *his* job is to stop sending flowers and writing poetry. He is to cease all flattering comments. He is to make an effort to be late for all dates (and then get angry at me for pressuring him and not accepting him the way he is). There is a lot of freedom inside the *job description* for those men who enjoy bringing some creativity into their tortures. *My* job is to grow an intense emotional bond with *him* based on his behavior from the first two months. I will expect the same amount of flowers and poetry (or at least a flattering comment). I will be disappointed when I don't get anything. At that point, I will become violently aware that *he* has a tremendous amount of "work" to do on himself. I have an important decision to make: Do I stick it out or move on to the next one?

Thus the Six Men Per Year Theory was born.

## SUNDAY MORNING REVIVAL

This morning finds me with yet another Romeo in my bed. I, of course, am sitting as far away as humanly possible. There are some serious drawbacks to living in a studio apartment.

As I sit at my faithful computer, a number of thoughts run through my foggy brain this morning. First I have to tell the kids in apartment two to wash the candy off their fingers before they use my keyboard. Second, I have to get a life that's at least partially based on reality. Why is this guy in my bed while I am sitting in a chair at 9:20 on a Sunday morning? What the hell is that all about? I secretly desire to wake him up, tell him to pack his shit, and toss the whole lot out the door. My mother taught me to be a gracious host, I guess.

Once again I am experiencing the sting of infidelity. Romeo, after only six months, screwed the pooch. Well, whoever she was, she has instantly been transformed into a bitch. Romeo screwed her. Thus, he screwed the pooch. *Jerk!*

As this person is comfortably lounging in *my bed,* I can see that he is lying on his well-muscled back. He is sleeping with his beautiful mouth open. I wonder if he would mind if I took this opportunity to pour lye down his deceitful little throat.

The sick thing is that I think this S.O.B. is actually feeling relieved to have the truth come out. Confession is good for the soul. I bet some goody-goody person wrote that. Whilst Romeo is basking in feelings of relief, Juliet over here is quietly plotting revenge. When you least expect it, expect it, Butthead. But for now, I must return to my magnanimous, understanding, gracious self. Damn, I'll probably make him breakfast. And if he tells me I'm pretty, I might even screw him good-bye.

## ONE WOMAN'S QUESTION TO HER FRIENDS

Why is it that all of you, my friends, wait until I've broken up with someone to share that you always knew that person was wrong for me? Why do you wait to relay a series of unforgivable incidences that *clearly* illustrated that that guy was very wrong for me? Why do you withhold this precious information until it doesn't matter anymore? I know you don't want to seem unsupportive, but the next time you see me with an asshole, don't assume I have the brains to figure it out on my own. Based on past results, I don't.

## PERCEPTIONS

I have long been aware that when I am down on myself; I see a distorted image when I look in the mirror. I know this is happening and recognize the lie. It's like Bulimia without the throwing up – warped and ugly. The other thing I watch for is warped and ugly images of those around me.

I had a date with a dear man. It was confronting, as he was very sweet and very open to a greater level of intimacy right out of the shoot. Within a day of our meeting, my image of this fellow was one of ugliness. I was sharing this image with my pal Damon on the phone one night. I explained that this man was completely unacceptable because he had "a little face." I mean his features were just too close together.

The more I dwelt, the smaller his face became. Within a day or two, he was grotesque and never going to get a call from me again. He wrote, he called; I cringed. I don't remember why I decided to see this small-faced guy again, but I did. I was so surprised to see a handsome man walk into the room. His head and face were well proportioned and everything was fine. I instantly realized what was going on. This time when he raved about how great I am, I simply shared how I felt about the accolades. If memory serves, I told him my anus was clenching tightly, and then provided a visual aid with my clenched hand. I needed to share how I felt about being set on a pedestal by a stranger. He was respectful and took it all in.

Today when I think of him, I see the handsome, well-groomed man that he really is. There is nothing wrong with this guy's head or face. So, I'm on the phone for another marathon conversation with Damon and I tell him what happened with "little-face guy" and Damon said, "I know what you what you did. You gave this guy a little head."

"I did not! He never took his pants off!"

Silence from Damon, then, "You gave him a little head."

Ohhhhh, you don't have to spoon feed me the punchline more than twice. I gave him a little face. I gave him a little ugliness. I gave him a little head.

And he didn't even get to cum.

## KATIE'S NO DEFAULT THEORY

When a couple breaks up, and one or both parties cannot find a suitable replacement in a comfortable period of time, the aforementioned parties do not automatically revert back to their original owners.

## MAYBE I SHOULD MARRY A GARBAGE MAN

It is not crucial to my happiness that all human beings like me. This is an important day in my life. Boy, when I think of all the wasted time spent trying to keep things friendly with my ex-lovers, I could puke.

Truth be known, I think I just wanted to save them in case I needed to have my needs met . . . or, until I found some other unsuspecting fool to take my garbage out.

## MORDANT'S PHILOSOPHICAL MOMENT

"I've had some great scenes in my life, but they ended up on the cutting room floor."

### TONY'S EPIPHANY

During a pre-movie chat, my male friend Tony had an epiphany. He announced that the difference between a young person and a person of experience is simple. A young person thinks in terms of *right now* whereas an experienced person thinks in terms of *forever.*

Nothing we haven't heard before, but valid just the same.

## I AM AWARE

I'm aware that there is some sort of problem. Not so much consciously, but let's just say there are signs. Here's an example:

I'm single. I love it. My time is my own. My apartment is furnished, impeccably, with *my* stuff. I know where everything is (except phone numbers 'cause they're on little pieces of paper all over my office). I come and go as I please, I check in with no one, I don't shave any more (sure sign I'm not getting laid), I wash my hair every three days, and I wear my hair in a bun most of the time. No make-up, no dieting, no douching. And best of all: no jealousy, insomnia, paranoia, or inferiority complex. I'm single and I love it.

*I love it so much I think I'd hunt down and kill anyone who tried to take my single status away.* This isn't good, I know.

The mere thought of some guy lying in my bed waiting for me when I get home makes me quake with fear. The thought of having some person in my life that wants to spend time with me daily is repulsive. I love waking up in the morning alone and hate knowing I should turn off the TV so *we* can get some sleep. I hate that warm and squishy look guys get on their face. This isn't good, I know.

See, right now there just isn't anything motivating me to change. Nothing except that gnawing feeling that I'm avoiding some important shit. I have this feeling that eating in front of the TV every night is bad. I have this feeling that *only* wanting to hang out with people who want *nothing* from me is somehow proof of some kind of dysfunction on my part. I have this feeling that it's not *normal* to see eight movies per week. I have this feeling that dreaming weekly about my now married-to-a-stripper ex-boyfriend is proof that I'm not OK. I have this feeling that literally running away when a man asks me for a date denotes an imbalance. I have this feeling that *All My Children* is not real, and that really breaks my heart.

# GIDGET'S BOY LIST
## Must Have (if you don't got it, you don't get it, baby!):

- Dependable and Trustworthy
- Trusting
- Will take care of me, and allow me to take care of him
- Empathetic
- Emotionally stable
- Lives within 20 miles of me
- Able to admit it when he's wrong
- Able to manage his money
- Will share
- Has an open mind
- Rarely, if ever, indulges in recreational pharmaceuticals
- As smart or smarter than me
- Will not ridicule me, or allow me to ridicule myself
- Usually a rule follower
- Reasonable
- Knows that yelling will *not* get his point across
- Will be my equal/my partner
- Will encourage, but not rush me
- Will give me space
- Self-motivated
- Optimistic
- Faithful
- A good friend
- Right kind of weird
- A person I can really talk to
- Dynamic, sexy, and passionate
- Polite
- Will appreciate me and notice my sacrifices
- I will make sacrifices
- Can be quite naughty
- A learner
- Gets along with my friends

## WONDERING
Do we always need someone to blame?  Just wondering.

## PSYCHO PHILOSOPHY
Leave 'em before they have a chance to leave you.

## A MORDANT-ISM
I want to get better, not *bitter.*

## A DAMON-ISM
When it's time to talk, it's time to walk.

## NOW
"Now" is the best time of my life. That's why they call it a *present.*

## SILLY JOKE FROM DAMON
You know how women are always yelling "Harder! Faster!"?
Well, sometimes I just want to yell back "Wetter! Tighter!"

## ONE WOMANS EXPERIENCE
I will probably regret writing this, but I think it's relevant. I know it's funny.

For the past few years I've been doing a lot of soul searching. After all that time, you'd think I would have learned something. I've been almost celibate. I've been practically dateless. I've been pretty happy. Almost. month ago, I decided to dip my toe in the old dating pool.

First, we have Hercules (Of course I changed the name, silly): Big, beautiful, smart, funny...and an ex-con. So, while the rest of us were boinking everything in sight during our twenties, Herc was locked up.

Like anyone, Herc had a couple of women lie and cheat on him. But again, while the rest of us were able to confront, holler at, dump, marry, and generally interact with these vile monsters, Herc was locked away, helpless to do anything but hear the stories about these hideous women. His family dynamics were terrifyingly dysfunctional. But, man, he sure was *purdy*!

So, I say to myself, "Self, here we have a man who is completely incapable of intimacy right now. He doesn't trust anyone. He's pissed off at humanity, especially women. He looked you dead in the eyes and told you he does not want a commitment." So, I had sex with him. Twice.

As I was crawling out of the bedroom at four in the morning praying Herc wouldn't wake up, I realized casual sex had lost its appeal in a big way. I suppose I would have told him I lost my contact or something if he would have woken up. Of course, it would have been weird since I don't even wear glasses. But, these are the risks you take in the old dating pool. I think I got about three hours of sleep before I had to get up and get ready for date number two.

This guy I have lovingly named the Dress-Wearing-Alien-Guy. To the gentleman in question: I know if you ever read this, you'll be pissed off. But honestly, honey, you really should be a bit more selective with whom you share your weirdness.

I had a very nice first date with the Dress-Wearing-Alien-Guy. It was with a group of wacky folks, and all had a good time. I consented to a second date. It was just the two of us until we joined his family for dinner. Again, all had a good time.

I called to confirm our third date and let him know that when he arrived at my home, my dog, Thor, would greet him at the door. He said that he had sort of a weird relationship with dogs and sounded a bit apprehensive. I assured him I would come to the door and there would be no problem.

It was then that this fellow informed me that dogs sense that he's not from around here. I innocently said, "Oh, you mean they can tell you're not from Minnesota?" "No," he replied. "I'm not from earth." Now, I realize I should have just hung up right then and there. But, *no*, idiot girl over here just came back with a snappy "Well . . . uh . . . Thor's got a pretty open mind. I'm sure he'll be just fine." And I confirmed our plans for Sunday's outing.

I didn't even set the receiver down. I instantly called a girlfriend – we'll call her Jen – and begged her to accompany me and the "Alien" to the Renaissance Festival that Sunday. I think she agreed just so she could get a gander at this guy. I couldn't have cared less. I just could not bear being alone with someone who may sprout tentacles and eat me.

He drove to the Festival as we ladies had already begun to partake in the fruit of the vine. He was a champ when I asked him if, as an alien, he had special powers. Everyone laughed and I was beginning to think I had misjudged this fellow. We had a great day and I invited both of them back to my place for a cocktail to finish off the date. That's when it got weird.

Apparently, my "alien" friend could not contain himself one more minute; can open, worms everywhere. Here's how it went down:

He mentioned that he was a massage therapist, and somehow managed to convince Jen and I that he could massage both of our feet at the same time (after all, we were walking all day). The maneuver involved we two ladies lying side by side so he could get to our feet easily. At one point, I remember turning my head to one side and looking at Jen. She could not stop laughing.

Then, in an inspiration of brilliance alien boy announces, "Gee, these pants sure are binding." Shit. "Do you have a dress I could borrow?" Now, in those days there was a five-minute fad, in which certain hippie boys would wear a long skirt instead of trousers. So, I gave him the benefit of the doubt and said, "You mean a skirt?"

"No," he replied. "I mean a dress. Maybe something light and floral."

At this point, Jen sat bolt upright and said, "Okay. I'm outta here. You're on your own." And she left.

All I can tell you is the evening got weirder and weirder. I forbade him to wear a dress in front of my roommates. At one point, I tried to pawn him off on a houseguest by telling my guest that this fellow gave a great foot massage. It may have worked except that the Dress-Wearing-Alien-Guy also could not stop mentioning that he had unusually bad body odor, apparently hereditary. I think that little massage lasted three minutes and crazy boy was back in my face.

Even when I flat out told him to leave, he remained. I even said, "You know that thought you have where there's you and me and sex – all in the same thought? Well, forget about it. It's never gong to happen."

Still, he remained on the auspices that he needed to sober up. I couldn't send this guy out to his death, so the torture continued. Jen could drive hours earlier, I was straight as an arrow, but apparently Dress-Wearing-Alien-Guys metabolize slower than humans.

Finally, hours after I showed obvious signs of revulsion, the Dress-Wearing-Alien-Guy was ready to depart. Of course, he had to do one more weird thing. Instead of trying to kiss me, he put one hand on my forehead and one on his own. I think I said something like, "What the hell are you doing?" The answer has something to do with the exchange of energy, and I let him know there would be none of that monkey business around here.

Honestly, it's enough to make a single gal marry!

## THE EMPTINESS
### (or Mordant's Moment of Clarity)
I think
that we have an emptiness
that we try to fill with other people.
That until we begin to
like ourselves
and become happy with who and what
we are,
we will always
keep on trying fill the void
with what we see in other people.
Only to find,
later,
that they cannot fix
what we are lacking.

## THE MIRROR
I looked into your
eyes
and then I saw
Myself,
myself,
myself,
myself,
my selves.

–Madame Rujah–

# OUR ~~12~~ 13-STEP PROGRAM FOR PULLING YOUR DATING LIFE TOGETHER

**(Clearly revised from the Alcoholics Anonymous 12 step program, with deepest gratitude)**

1.    We realize that we have total control over our dating lives. That we are the author/creator of all our relationship situations, whether through the actions we take or the permission(s) we give.

2.    Come to believe that we can make the changes necessary to restore sanity to our dating life and develop healthy relationships.

3.    Make the decision to seize control of our lives. Take the steps necessary to do so: education, introspection, and practice...to the point where healthy relationships become the paradigm.

4.    Make a searching and fearless inventory of ourselves. Trusting that this is for our greater good, we boldly seek out the light and the dark that makes us who we are.

5.    Own up to the dysfunction we discover in self-examination. Admit the exact nature of our wrongs to ourselves and the Universe, or at least a close girlfriend, knowing that we are a work in progress and that this is a necessary step on the road to a greater level of intimacy.

6.    Reach that point where we are totally ready to remove all these barriers to intimacy.

7.    Ask for help – from our Higher Self/the Universe/God or a good therapist – in removing obstacles keeping us from attaining true happiness with intimacy.

8.    Make a list of all hurtful attributes and commit to treating our intimate partners and ourselves and with kindness and respect.

9.    Forgive others and ourselves for their ignorant behavior.

10.    Continue to keep vigilantly aware of our actions and their consequences, looking at missteps not as sins or failures, but as opportunities to learn.

11.    Through affirmations, meditation, and/or prayer, improve our conscious contact with our highest selves and subsequently our concept of our higher power – whether it be God, the Universe, or Prada – seeking knowledge of our true dating/relationship path and the strength of will to stay on it.

12.    Having had an epiphany and consequent breakthrough as a result of what we have learned, we carry this message of hope to our closest friends still floundering in the shallow end of the gene pool. We continue to set the example, putting these principles to practice in all our affairs...so to speak.

13.    Continue to seek out ways to better ourselves through books, conversations, seminars, DVDs, CDs, and/or therapy, constantly continuing our education; always growing and co-creating the fabulous person we see ourselves to be.

–**R. Mordant Mahon & Sarina Stone**–

www.ingramcontent.com/pod-product-compliance
Lightning Source LLC
Chambersburg PA
CBHW071133280326
41935CB00010B/1210